Pierre de Lano

Napoleon III. and Lady Stuart

An episode of the Tuileries

Pierre de Lano

Napoleon III. and Lady Stuart
An episode of the Tuileries

ISBN/EAN: 9783337350468

Printed in Europe, USA, Canada, Australia, Japan

Cover: Foto ©ninafisch / pixelio.de

More available books at **www.hansebooks.com**

NAPOLEON III. AND

LADY STUART

AN EPISODE OF THE TUILERIES

TRANSLATED FROM THE FRENCH
OF

PIERRE DE LANO

BY

A. C. S.

NEW YORK
J. SELWIN TAIT & SONS
65 FIFTH AVENUE
1894

COPYRIGHT, 1895,
BY
J. SELWIN TAIT & SONS,
NEW YORK.

All Rights Reserved.

PREFACE.

Some years ago, I happened to meet a lady in a Parisian *salon*, who was very prominent at the Tuileries, towards the close of the reign of Napoleon III., whose personality I have already cursorily sketched in my works on the Second Empire.

I enquired about her and ascertained that after the disaster of 1870, she had gone abroad, but had returned to France at the close of the war and established herself in Paris.

Knowing that this lady had, not long before, been very intimate with Napoleon III., and had been one of his closest friends, after having been introduced to her, I determined to learn from her personally, the particulars of the incident which I am about to relate.

This event in her life, of which particulars are given in the following pages is in no sense a commonplace one, and possesses all the interest of the most dramatic novel.

I found her willing to aid me in the vindication of her character, and to give me the benefit of her recollections, without which it would have been impossible for me to write this book.

This woman, whom I shall call Lady Stuart, was very nearly of the same age as the Empress Eugénie, whose rival she was, and has, to-day, like her, white hair. She formerly enjoyed all the privileges of an acknowledged beauty, and held a high and envied position, but she suffered cruelly.

It is her cry of anguish—born of pride, of love and maternity—which will find an echo in these pages.

P. de L.

NAPOLEON III. AND LADY STUART:

AN EPISODE OF THE TUILERIES.

CHAPTER I.

AT THE TUILERIES.

In 1866, after Sadowa, when the Emperor Napoleon III. had declared his inability to restrain the ambitious designs of Prussia, the inscrutability, which ordinarily characterized his features, seemed to have abandoned him, and he was unable to conceal the anxiety which was preying upon his mind.

The Court for a long time had been made up of the scheming and empty-headed courtiers who formed the usual retinue of the Empress Eugénie, and the men and women in their intercourse with their sovereign feigned ignorance of the attitude of the Emperor, for fear that they might be obliged to abandon their habitual round of pleasures.

In spite of the systematic course of gaiety prevailing at the Court, the bitterness which filled the mind of Napoleon III. was too evident, either to be denied or ignored. There were, however, among the courtiers a few who were sufficiently alive to the interests of their country or animated with the desire to concern themselves with the political clouds which were threatening on the frontiers to feel oppressed with uneasiness and apprehension.

In the uncertainty of those anxious days, some of the more circumspect and prudent waited with good taste the signal from their sovereign to abandon themselves again to their habitual pleasures, or for such circumstances as might indicate to them the proper attitude to assume. But others who were less hypocritical or more devoted to a life of sensual gratification, loudly deplored the dullness which prevailed at the Court, and protested that it was wrong to listen to these bearers of evil omens, and with a brutality not altogether free from a picturesque

egotism, did not hesitate to declare that the
"*patron*," was becoming a bore with his melancholy ideas. These men and women who
were afterwards destined to find themselves
united in the desire for a war with Prussia
were unconsciously precipitating their own ruin
as well as that of their country. The "*patron*"
bored them then, as he would bore them later
when he attempted vainly to oppose the disastrous campaign for which they clamored.

They were the most violent and the most
imperious in 1866, as they were the most imperious and the most violent in 1870 and succeeded in convincing the advisers of the sovereigns that the anticipated dangers were imaginary, that the reluctance and sadness of the
Emperor meant nothing serious, and that it
was even policy in spite of the gravity of the
situation in Europe, to affect carelessness and
gaiety.

This carelessness was practised at the Tuileries after Sadowa and the courtiers amused
themselves thoroughly and the customary succession of fêtes went on without intermission.

The time was then drawing near for the *Exposition Universelle* of 1867, and it was desired that the inauguration of this Exposition should have a special *éclat*, should be in fact the apotheosis of the Imperial Court.

From that time, all obstacle to pleasure having disappeared, the men became more gallant or witty, according to their tastes, elegant dancers or impassioned lovers; the women cast to the winds the scruples which they had for a time simulated, and pressed with increased eagerness in the steps of the Empress or her most favored adherents.

At this time, *i.e.* towards the end of the year 1866, at one of the *fêtes* given at the Tuileries, Lady Stuart, by which name I shall refer to her, whose history I am going to relate in these pages, made her first appearance at Court.

Lady Stuart, who soon became known at the *Château*, by the more familiar and intimate name of the Countess Ellen, had already left her native country, England, and had established herself in Paris.

At that time, properly speaking, she had no history; however, aside from the notoriety which she had gained by her beauty and grand style of living in London—a notoriety which every great *mondaine* acquires as a matter of course—there was a sort of mystery in her life and this mystery, imperfectly guessed at and badly understood, added to her attractions in the eyes of the *habitués* of the Tuileries, as well as in those of the aristocratic society of that period.

Scandal-mongers or calumniators had endeavored to spread a story about her, saying that she was an ostracized woman who had fled from a society wearied of her charms, that she was a high-class adventuress foisted upon the Parisian world and the Imperial *salons*, in the interests of the British government. But these reports were only timidly whispered. As a matter of fact, Lady Stuart was of too good a family to permit a rash belief in the stories of which she was the object; besides being in too good odor at the British Embassy to allow of her playing the political *rôle* of which she was suspected.

The proverb says that there is never smoke without fire. This proverb might have been applied to Lady Stuart, and if the lovers of tittle-tattle and intrigues were not entirely correct in their facts in speaking of her, there were some indications which might have led them to this belief.

Tall, slender, very dark and very beautiful, remarkable above all for the beauty of her shoulders and her arms, which according to the expression of an admirer, or a lover perhaps, must have been bestowed upon her by the devil, she made her *entrée* at the Tuileries like a marvellous apparition from Fairyland, and from the moment of her arrival evoked a sincere enthusiasm among the courtiers.

Speaking French with a real purity of diction, and almost without any accent, she at once raised herself to a level far above the mob of exotic feminity which crowded the *salons* of the Empress, and took her station among the foremost ladies of the Court circle.

Although her establishment in Paris might almost be called modest, she never seemed to

miss the greater magnificence of her existence
in London, and proudly bore what some whispered was her ruin but which they never would
have dared to call her downfall.

Her past, imperfectly known, was simple.

Descended in an almost direct line from the
last kings of Ireland, she had united herself
in marriage to Lord Stuart, one of the highest
noblemen in the British peerage, but her married life had not been happy.

Very autocratic herself, she chafed at the
absolute autocracy of her husband, and after
living together for some years without the supreme and often redeeming consolation of a
child, she separated from him, only returning to
his side to fulfil those social obligations which
are so imperative among the English.

It seemed as if the uncongenial life which
had thus been made for her, could never change
for the better, when an accident changed her
whole existence.

Lord Stuart was found one morning dead
in bed. As he had retired the night before in
excellent health, had never suffered from heart

or brain troubles, and as the physicians who were summoned under the circumstances, did not know to what cause to attribute his death, the world was astonished and suspicious; and if the young wife who did not seem to grieve in the least for the loss of her husband escaped open and vulgar scandals, a mystery surrounded her—this mystery which was to excite so much malice in Paris.

Lady Stuart, however, did not disquiet herself about the attitude of society towards her after the death of her husband.

She had insisted on an autopsy being held, and as the hostile examination of science proved fruitless to discover any grounds of suspicion she had resolutely defied the threats which confronted her.

The death of Lord Stuart, however, was easily explained and resulted from very well-known causes.

Violently in love with his wife, and keenly alive to her superb physical charms, the excitement of their last meeting had precipitated an attack of apoplexy which proved fatal.

The young wife explained the sudden death of her husband as due to undue excitement, and it is wise, even just perhaps, to accept her version without question.

Free, henceforth, Lady Stuart lost no time in arranging for her new existence and the long-desired independence which her widowhood conferred upon her.

She wound up her affairs, realized her fortune and traveled. When she returned to London, the suspicions which had attached to her name had subsided. She became audacious; she presented herself at some of the houses which formerly were always open to her power and her beauty, and although at first there was some surprise, the world soon received her as before, and around her and for her it was again a modernized history of Panurge and his sheep. People appeared to have forgotten the mysterious death of Lord Stuart and the world paid her homage.

She might have profited by the situation, reopened her house in London and have resumed her life of the year before. But this was not her intention. Having received from English society, the circle to which she belonged, a justification and a rehabilitation, she did not linger in her own country, and announced soon that she had resolved to take up her residence in France, at Paris.

It was about the month of September, 1866 —that year so fruitful in dramatic events and mournful presages—that Lady Stuart first occupied a charming hotel in the Champs-Elysées.

The greater part of those who saw her establishment, saw nothing in her arrival but the advent of a beautiful and free woman, upon whom it would be agreeable to smile; they saw nothing in her but a coquette fascinated with the life of Paris. The rumors which represented her as a political spy, found but few listeners, and these shrugged their shoulders incredulously.

CHAPTER II.

As a matter of fact no one could know the reason that actuated Lady Stuart in taking a position in the Parisian world, and neither those who affected in their ignorance to consider her as a woman simply devoted to pleasure, or those who supposed her to be playing the *rôle* of a political spy, had any certain knowledge.

The first care of the young lady after having established herself in her new dwelling, was to request the British Ambassador to take steps for her presentation at the Tuileries, not the ordinary and easily obtained admission, of which so many were granted for the solemn receptions which took place two or three times a year, but a personal and special presentation, which could not be forgotten.

In acting thus Lady Stuart had an end in view and was following out the course which she had laid down for herself.

Very ambitious, very haughty, fond of power and undisputed homage, when she married Lord Stuart she had hoped that on account of the high position in which her marriage would place her she would shine in the front rank of the women of the English aristocracy. This hope had been realized in part; but that which she loved above all, that which she passionately desired: to rule others as much by the power of her beauty, as by the sovereignty of a real social supremacy, had been denied to her. She had desired that her husband should be one of the great officers of the State; she had wished to be the dreaded and envied companion of a statesman. But the noble lord insisted, in spite of her tears and reproaches, to decline any official position, or to take part in the affairs of his country, and she thought this disappointment of her plans a cruel deception.

In coming to Paris, she had determined to begin her life anew and to live according to the plans which she had formerly determined upon in her own mind.

But we cannot say that she acted upon any clearly-defined plan of action; nor can it be affirmed that any particular choice determined her conduct. But she was beautiful, rich and clever, and there were so many feared and envied men at that time, who were drifting on the tide of fortune towards unknown destinies,.

that she thought one of them might be cast at her feet by a chance wave, one who would bewitch her, one who would aid her in the proud realization of her desires and ambition, in that which had hitherto been but a chimera.

She disdained to be only a woman of fashion, of whom the world would talk for a day or a week, whose memory would soon fade in that Parisian fog in which so many beautiful women, so many charming shadows, passionate or cold—brunettes or blondes,—are lost, and who follow one another like an unending procession of ephemeral apparitions in a stereopticon.

She had no desire to be a female politician in the service of her country, one of those equivocal personalities who are only approached with caution, and whose favor is dreaded as a shameful evil.

She wished to be herself—herself, simply, but absolutely. She wished to be the friend— wife or mistress, she would not have been able to say which,—of a man who would have sufficient moral force and reputation to give her a high position in the eyes of the world—in the regular or irregular order of things—as an envied woman—whose hate was feared and friendship sought.

And in the conception of her dream, she did not ask herself whether the strongest affections and passions are durable and do not soon decline and cease to exist ; if the radiant promises of the hours which saw their birth are not followed by the fatal overthrow of the deepest and most fondly cherished hopes. She had a goal and saw but this goal, she smiled in the insolence of her beauty, intoxicated with the certainty of the arrival of that favorable opportunity, which would give her the spring-time of life, and gratify the ambition which had once been stifled under the gloomy London sky.

In every aspect of her character Lady Stuart appeared to be, physically and morally, an adventuress. But in her own house, this character of adventuress, even, was not exempt from a certain grandeur. Although an egoist as are all noble natures, she thought no evil: her great desire for the gratification of her ambition had nothing shameful in it, and as she did not confide it to the outside world, it would, indeed, be too puritanical to blame her for her designs.

The period at which Lady Stuart first made her appearance as a new and brilliant constellation in the firmament of the Parisian and Imperial festivities, was propitious for the fulfillment of her dream.

It really seemed then as if a young, beautiful and clever woman, had only to wish to be loved, to have the wish divined and gratified: she had only to single out a man among all those who fluttered in a whirl of thoughtlessness and pleasure, at the foot of the throne, and the fortunate individual would cast himself at her feet.

Paris and the Court, for those who only desired to make love and had nothing but love to offer in return, was full of young fools who devoted themselves to an elegant and amorous life, and with as much ardor as does a *belle* to her daily toilet.

Whilst in Paris there was an incessant orgy

of cloying sensual pleasure; it was at the Court that the wildest license prevailed. Notwithstanding the fact that the Empress herself remained uncontaminated amid all these temptations, first encouraging and then driving to the verge of despair those who had the misfortune to conceive a passion for herself, she ruled over this tumultuous crowd like an ancient idol, indifferent to the mass of victims offered at its shrine, and smiled alike at the misery of those who lacked success in this love chase, and the overweening vanity of those who triumphed.

Nearly every woman who was brought in contact with this rabble, was destined beforehand for ruin, was in fact, lost, and belonged no longer to herself. A peculiar atmosphere existed then at the Tuileries. Pathological observers declare that when a man, sound in body and mind, is subjected to a certain influence, as regards unaccustomed and surrounding scenes, he can—and often will,—succumb to the influences to which he is subjected, to the scenes by which he is surrounded. These observers

affirm, for instance, that a perfectly sane man,
can and even must go mad if he is compelled to
consort with madmen. This physiological and
psychological phenomenon was exemplified at
the Tuileries, among the women who were the
habitual frequenters of the Court. Exposed to
the scarcely concealed desires of the men, and
the atmosphere of feverish sensuality which
prevailed at the Château, and which intoxicated
their poor little frivolous souls, as much as
though they had already yielded, they no
longer had the power to resist, and had not the
strength to offer a serious defense ; the instinct
of modesty, which is so strong with women,
even though fallen beyond redemption, abandoned them and in a weak moment they fell.

There were certainly at the Tuileries and I
wish to repeat it once more, women who were
above reproach, who were unmoved by the
solicitations of those who desired their favors,
as there are in spite of the assertions of *savants*,
people who, although they live with madmen,
remain sane : but these women could rely upon
themselves, and did not really belong to those

who were justly called, the "*Women of the Tuileries.*"

Lady Stuart—the Countess Ellen—when she appeared at the Court, found naturally enough that she was besieged by these Don Juans who devoted themselves indefatigably to love-making. But she was of a different nature to that which characterized the women with whom she was to associate, and knew how to be deaf to appeals, and to keep herself free from reproach.

Destiny had in store for her a more exalted intrigue, than the commonplace ones which sprang up and died every day at the Tuileries and was more cruel to her than to those who had nothing to weep for but the short duration of an intrigue.

In gaining access to the Tuileries she had resolved to pay no attention to the exclusively worldly element among the men, an element which was in high favor in the circle of the Empress.

She knew that among these pleasure-loving men there were others, not less attractive, who devoted themselves to the nobler and more intellectual ambition of achieving power and station. She knew that these men hovered around the Emperor and it was on them that she decided to concentrate her efforts.

The ministerial and diplomatic circles of that day were composed of men who were nearly all of the highest rank and most brilliant intellect.

It mattered little to Lady Stuart, whether the man who should realize her beautiful dream of the year before, and should make her what she earnestly desired,—a successful woman—was French or a foreigner.

Like the Empress before her—that Empress whose every desire was to-day, fulfilled,—she wished to leave far behind her, with a hatred of her unlucky lot up to the present time, the ostentatious vanities of her former existence, in order that she might raise herself above other women, and rule them with all the power of her intellect. Like the Empress again, she entered the lists with a smile on her face, equal to any fortune, and indifferent whether the magician who should draw her from her comparative obscurity were young or old; whether ambassador, minister, prince or king,—provided that this magician made his appearance, and placed the magic potion to her lips which would transfigure her.

CHAPTER III.

THE morality of Lady Stuart was certainly not in conformity with that which directs or appears to direct ordinary humanity. But as it was developed in all its cynical frankness at a Court which was but little inspired by the austere principles which are binding upon the world generally—that honest world which hears without noticing, and which looks without seeing—her morality was not altogether without excuse and was even in a sense, logical.

It was at a fête given in the winter of 1866, that Lady Stuart leaning on the arm of the British Ambassador, entered the Tuileries.

She looked marvellously beautiful and created
a sensation. Old courtiers as they looked at
her almost believed themselves carried back to
the days when the Comtesse de Castiglione contrasted her classic beauty with the not less perfect beauty of the Empress, and haughtily and
triumphantly passed through the ranks of the
agitated courtiers.

The greater part of the women—a flatterer
would say all the women—who formed the
usual circle of the Empress, were lovely, but
to the Comtesse de Castiglione and Lady Stuart
was unanimously awarded the palm for pre-
eminence in beauty.

It is well known that in order to see the
Comtesse de Castiglione, when she passed
through the *salons* at Court, all etiquette was
forgotten, the courtiers crowded, and jostled
one another, and even stood on the benches,
covered with red velvet and embroidered in
gold, which lined the walls, and formed a hedge
around her as if she had been a Queen.

Lady Stuart was received with the same
enthusiasm and the same murmur of admiration,

and she was promptly and prettily nicknamed the "Countess Ellen"—when she made her appearance at Court in the company of the distinguished statesman who presented her.

There was such a crush in her direction when she entered supported by her escort, on the way to the *salon* where the Emperor and Empress were, that the ambassador was obliged to stop and wait until he was permitted to continue on his way.

In spite of the sudden block caused by the sensational appearance of the young lady, her escort smiled and leaning towards her said in English:—

"People here are accustomed to seeing handsome women, but notwithstanding madame, as you see, they are astounded at your beauty."

In the presence of this new arrival, a possible object for their pursuit, the men were enraptured and those who were the most famous for their gallantry, and for success in their intrigues, promptly marked her for their own.

The women were very uneasy at sight of the beautiful English woman, and formed an alliance against her with a sort of instinct of self-preservation, from the first moment of her appearance. They divined that this new comer belonged to the class of conquerors, and that she would require her share—a large share—in the pleasure which was lavished upon them daily. So jealous were they of her that they were scarcely able to refrain from showing their feelings, being restrained from doing so, only by the usages of polite society, and they received her with the coldness of antagonists ready for the fray.

However, the presentation of Lady Stuart to the Emperor and Empress had been distinguished by too much favor from royalty, to permit of the young woman being openly slighted, and as the Duchesse de Bassano Lady-of-Honor to the Empress, who was sometime after succeeded by Comtesse Walewska, made honeyed speeches to her—a thing of which she was somewhat chary—people understood that it was better perhaps to accept with at least a semblance of favor the new star which had risen in the firmament of the Tuileries, but that it would also be better not to proffer their assistance in securing her an influential position at Court, a place which she seemed well able to gain for herself in spite of all opposition and hostility.

Lady Stuart was not the first one who had been the object of the envy of the ladies of the Court. Each time that a prepossessing woman attempted to force herself into the circle of their intimacies or worldly pleasures, they treated her as an enemy, organized petty conspiracies against her and threw every obstacle in the way of the *débutante*. If, then, the woman so received, was either timid or sensitive she was frightened and discouraged, gave up the idea of becoming a member of the charmed circle as either illusory or too difficult of attainment, and retired leaving the field free for her adversaries. But if the woman who found herself confronted with all those petty meannesses which can be concocted in a feminine coterie bent upon malicious mischief, was a daring and determined opponent, she was not long in silencing evil tongues, in breaking up coalitions, and in taking her place among those whose position was assured, feared as she was, all the more for having bravely withstood the attack made upon her.

This ought to have been the case with Lady Stuart, but to tell the truth she met with but few difficulties at the Château, in accurately defining her position, for the women composing the circle of the Empress were quick to perceive that she was not one of those who is easily repulsed, or ignored as insignificant.

Women, to whatever grade of society they belong, are like collegians, hostile to a new professor or a freshman. Collegians test a freshman or professor by hazing him or playing practical jokes upon him. If the victim remains passive, resigned and submissive, he will have no peace. Tortures are reserved for him in the future which will wring shouts and tears from him. But if the man thus put to the test proves to be a sturdy antagonist and resents the treatment he receives, he will lead by the nose the pack which formerly howled at his heels.

Such are women in their relations with men and in their contact with their sisters. They fear or love those who defy them and humiliate them, losing even, in their enforced amiability, the recollection of the time when they were leagued against the man or woman who is now their acknowledged leader.

CHAPTER IV.

ON the night of the presentation of Lady Stuart at the Tuileries, there was one of those delicious fêtes, at which all the guests usually lost in the promiscuous gathering at the great official receptions, recognized one another and met on the common ground constituted by a similarity of tastes and sentiments.

Mmes. de Metternich, de Pourtalès, de Gallifet, Drouyn de Lhuys, de Chasseloup-Laubat, Péreira, Bartholoni, de Persigny, and many others, surrounded the admired and radiant Empress like a border of blooming flowers, in their light and many-hued *toilettes*, enhanced by the glitter of the jewels which flashed on their bosoms or were twined in their hair.

A perfect galaxy of men, worldlings, and statesmen, hovered around them, or, broken up into groups, chatted as they walked through the *salons*.

The Emperor, with his usual heavy and deliberate step, musing with eyelids downcast, from beneath which he flashed an occasional glance, and pulling his mustache, came and went among the crowd, vouchsafing a word to a particular friend, smiling on a woman abashed at finding herself suddenly in front of him, while still perchance, agitated by the memory of a recent intimacy, long sought, quickly passed, and without a morrow.

The men were dressed *à la française*, in black coats, carrying under their arms black felt cocked hats, profusely trimmed with silk braid, court swords at their sides. They wore knee breeches, shoes with silver buckles, and were attired similarly to Napoleon III., who only donned the uniform of General of Division on the occasion of grand receptions when the representatives of Commerce, Industry and Finance were admitted to the Court. The effect gave the *salons* a tone of sombre, colorless, subdued elegance, which was relieved by the brilliancy and splendor of the military uniforms, and of those of the officers as well as of the Chamberlains of the Tuileries.

The costume of the Chamberlains was in truth superb. It consisted of a red coat, *à la française*, embroidered with gold, waistcoat and trousers of white satin, white silk stockings, a cocked hat with white feathers, and sword for the Emperor's household. The only difference in the uniform for the household of the Empress was a light blue coat.

Lady Stuart although she had seen the magnificence at the English Court, where the dresses are those which were in fashion in the days of Henry VIII., was dazzled when she was suddenly confronted with the many-colored crowd which filled the Tuileries.

Having been invited by the Empress to take her place in her "circle," she seated herself and conversed with the sovereign as well as with the ladies who accompanied her.

This conversation. according to the Countess

Ellen, who here confirms what I have already stated, regarding feminine gossip at the Tuileries, was, that evening, what it always was— trivial or sometimes animated by a sudden spasm of gaiety excited by some anecdote or frivolous remarks, the anecdotes always referring to the scandal of the city and the *boudoirs*, and the remarks applying to the male element concerned.

Lady Stuart had occupied for some time the seat to which the Empress had invited her, when the Emperor advanced towards what was called, "the women's corner," more irreverently, the "seraglio," or the "alcove," and having spoken to some of the ladies, turned to the new arrival. Then in the low drawling voice which characterized him, he said to her:

"Would it be agreeable to you, madame, to make the tour of the *salons* with me?"

And with a smile qualifying such a trivial and commonplace observation, he added:

"This is what people in France call the walk of the master of the house, when he is at home and has a pretty woman leaning on his arm. We have the tour of the *salons*, the tour of the waltz, the tour of the lake, in truth we have all kinds of tours."

The women who heard this somewhat commonplace wit of the Emperor and his execrable attempt at a pun, laughed approvingly.

But the Empress, who was watching her husband, and who seemed uneasy, broke in on the merriment, with the remark:

" There are also the naughty tours, sire; has your Majesty overlooked them?"

Napoleon III. looked very calmly at his companion, and replied:

" I have not forgotten them, but pass them by as they are no longer for us."

And graciously addressing himself to the listening ladies, he added:

" Isn't that the case, ladies?"

These words were spoken lightly, but those who knew the relations existing between the Empress and her husband, foresaw the near approach of a quarrel.

The Empress in fact had never been able to reconcile herself to her husband's gallantries with the habitual frequenters of the Tuileries, and above all with those who were new arrivals at the Court, and terrible scenes occurred between the Emperor and Empress, caused by a light word whispered in a coquettish ear, at a *soirée*.

Lady Stuart, however, rose without appearing to understand the annoyance of the Empress, and placing her arm within that of the Emperor, she smilingly walked away with him, much gratified by the honor paid her, and enjoying the surprise evinced by the guests, who, equally astonished at the unwonted honor conferred by Napoleon III. on this woman, bowed before her as she passed, already seeing in her a favorite whose influence might be useful to them.

The English ambassador and the Duke de Persigny, who were chatting together at the time, saw the couple majestically glide past them.

M. de Persigny paused abruptly in what he was saying, and frowning, said:

"I compliment you my Lord, you have, or rather others are gaining for you, all the honors of the evening."

The diplomatist who knew the brusqueness

of M. de Persigny, simply smiled and without remarking on the stress which the former had laid on the word "others," replied:

"I assure you, Duke, that I have not sought them. You are too suspicious, and you should sometimes think of our old device:—'*Honi soit qui mal y pense.*'"

Whilst M. de Persigny and the noble lord were holding this conversation, MM. de Metternich and Nigra who had been inseparable and unwearying in their attentions to each other since Sadowa, were chatting as they watched the Emperor and Lady Stuart.

All of a sudden, M. de Metternich murmured in a low voice, "Isn't it strange about that woman?"

"No," observed M. de Nigra, "she is only a woman, and is playing her part as a woman. She is doing it well, that is all."

"What, do you think——?"

"I think nothing, but would you like me to tell you a fable?"

"Tell it."

"You are aware that a popular superstition

says that when you see a shooting star at night, you should make a vow. Now, what vow would you make in the presence of this woman passing us?"

"You embarrass me."

"Well, I will answer for you. I would swear never to love her."

"It is for the Emperor that you say this?"

"Yes and no. Isn't the Emperor in love with all women?"

M. de Metternich looked as if he were joking, as he said:

"You should be the last, Nigra, to blame him for that."

M. Nigra's eyes flashed. "I beg your pardon," he said a little nervously, "as far as I am concerned, I don't love all women."

M. de Metternich, who was hopelessly in love with the Empress Eugénie, and who was well aware of the passion of the young sovereign for his colleague, and the indifference with which he had always viewed her preference, bit his lips and changed the conversation to a less delicate subject.

While this was going on, Lady Stuart, who was afterwards informed by the Ambassador of Austria, of the conversation that he had with Nigra, continued her stroll around the *salons* with the Emperor.

Napoleon III., who did not talk much when in the company of men, became animated in the presence of a beautiful woman. This evening he was very gracious with Lady Stuart.

Walking very slowly, he conversed with her, and listened to her replies, happy to forget the cares of his station, and making the most of the pleasant time at his disposal.

As the Emperor loved all women, according to the somewhat sarcastic remark of M. Nigra, he was easily beguiled by any attractive person, who could, in consequence, boast of the delight —even though ephemeral—of knowing him intimately.

Lady Stuart who was surpassingly beautiful, had an easy task with him, and if she had only desired the joy and pride which contented so many other women, it would not have taken long to realize her wishes.

But the Emperor when in her society experienced an uneasiness and a charm which was not altogether attributable to the senses.

Napoleon III., habitually derived more physical than mental pleasure from his love affairs. Notwithstanding this he had some lasting *liaisons* which were not entirely dependent upon animal passion. He loved some women, only a few it is true, for reasons other than their physical charms, among whom were Mme. de Castiglione, Mme. de Mercy-Argenteau, and one or two others whom I will not name. Clever women, they carried on with the Emperor not only a love affair, but an exchange of wit, and it is safe to say that if he was so much attached to them, it was attributable to a great extent to the charms of their minds displayed in their relations with him.

It would not be unnatural to wonder that Napoleon III. counted so few women remarkable for their intellect among his favorites, since he encouraged the introduction to him of women who were his equals intellectually.

In fact, it appears that the Emperor was far

from desiring only the gratification of his sensual impulses, and had systematically eliminated it from his life. The reason of this is easy to explain.

The Empress Eugénie had wearied her husband by an intimacy free from true passion, full of unpleasantnesses and scoldings, and had caused him to become distrustful of women, a foe to effusion of any kind, and to dread the direct contact of his mind with that of a woman.

Disappointed in his conjugal hopes, he had flitted from brunette to blonde, according to the whim of the moment, desirous of finding in this sort of indiscriminate love-making, the gratification of his dominant impulses, and oblivion for the hurts which his wife had already inflicted and still continued to inflict upon him.

He had demanded only from a woman the sweetness and emotion of her sex, and had wished for nothing more.

However, his intellect had caused him to depart from this course in two or three instances. Thus had arisen his *liaisons* with Mme. de

Castiglione, and Mme. de Mercy-Argenteau—this last lady having nearly run her course as a beauty—and Lady Stuart might have been one of those who whilst he feared them, he had not the strength of mind to repulse, when he met them unexpectedly, in the unforeseen events of his life.

During this evening, his conversation with the Countess Ellen was trivial and commonplace and she followed his example.

However, he questioned her, and found out what he desired to know. He saw that she was a wonderful conversationalist, as well as an extremely clever woman, and I would add, if I did not fear to be impertinent that when he led her back to her seat, he was conquered.

His last remark as he left her was insinuating: it was one of those speeches for which some women would have ruined themselves, if he had addressed it to them.

"I hope that the Tuileries please you madam," said the Emperor to his companion.

"Very much, sire," was the reply of the Countess Ellen.

And she added :— "The Emperor having deigned to honor me with his friendship, why should it not be pleasing to me?"

A pale, inscrutable smile—that inscrutable, pale smile which hovered so often on the lips of the sovereign, rested on Napoleon's mouth, and with a friendly gesture he murmured:

"In that case, madam, I count on seeing you again."

Then, with a slow and even step he left her and mingled with some of the groups which were scattered through the *salons*.

If Lady Stuart was feeling triumphant at the success of her *début*, no one would have known it from her manner as she composedly joined the ladies in the circle of the Empress.

She even feigned not to notice the whisperings, and the looks which were directed at her, and preserving a friendly demeanor towards all, she seemed to consider the honor which the sovereign had paid her, a very natural thing and of no importance.

Even the Empress, suspicious as she was, feeling reassured by her calmness, received her graciously, and when at the end of the evening, the English Ambassador gave her his arm to lead her away, her triumph was complete.

As she left the room, one of the *habitués* of the Tuileries made a remark characteristic of the philosophy professed at the Court—regarding the reception of the young woman at the Tuileries, and the favor shown her.

Winking significantly, he whispered in a low voice in the ear of a friend, in the somewhat cynical license of language in use at the Château:

"One more for the '*patron*' to-day: one more for us to-morrow. Now is the time to make your game!"

The man addressed, shrugged his shoulders.

"I think you are mistaken," said he. "I was watching that woman. Assuredly she will be for the '*patron*' but for no one else. With her, my friend, the game is made, and '*rien ne va plus.*'"

In the court-yard of the Tuileries, in front of the façade looking on the gardens, the carriages belonging to the principal invited guests were drawn up, the coachmen and footmen being grouped around enormous braziers, which blazed up and lent a reddish hue to the darkness of the night.

As Lady Stuart made her appearance and walked towards the Ambassador's carriage, her radiant beauty was lit up by the light.

The Ambassador said to her: "Have you amused yourself to-night madam?"

The young lady made a vague gesture. "*Amused* myself, my lord," she replied, "I was *interested*."

And she glided into the darkness of the *coupé*, which was rapidly whirled away by the impatient horses.

CHAPTER V.

A FAVORITE.

LADY STUART in answering the English Ambassador, by saying that she had simply been interested by what she had seen and heard, was clever, for she had thus indicated her unwillingness to reveal the exact condition of her mind. She did not think it expedient, at that time to disclose the sentiments by which she might be inspired, or to appear to know those which she had inspired.

She had, in truth, been more than interested during the evening which she had passed at the Château, and if she had entered it uncertain and as if committed to the current of events, as if questioning the circumstances which were to decide her fortune more or less rapidly, she left it joyously intoxicated with all the mad hope of a dream which had appeared unattainable to so many women.

In the success which had carried her almost giddily to the highest position among all those ladies assembled that evening around the sovereigns, she had a distinct apprehension of her situation, and among all the men who had smiled on her and bowed to her, she had only seen and had only wished to see one man—the Emperor. At one prodigious leap, her hope, her ambition, her pride had attained a height from which she determined they should not descend.

The Emperor appeared to her as he always was, good-natured, gracious, polite, although a little gloomy. He had paid her marked attention and she was sufficiently familiar with courts to know that she might expect anything from this special mark of favor.

The Emperor was not displeasing to her. He knew how to charm when he wished, and he had tried to fascinate her. However, the impression which he had made on her was but slight: recalling the *tête-à-tête* which she had had with him, she only felt and only desired to feel one thing, and that was, that Napoleon III. would fall in love with her if she encouraged him to do so later on.

This, for her was the important question: should she yield to the prayers of the Emperor, and become like so many others who had preceded her, his mistress?

She knew the enormous facility which characterized love intrigues at the Tuileries. She knew that the greater part of the women who

yielded to the sovereign, who responded to his
appeal, were no sooner discarded, than they
were snapped up. She was indignant at the
thought of being treated like one of these
women, and although she continued firm in her
determination to gain the affections of Napoleon III., she was puzzled to devise some
means by which she might be something more
for him than the mere plaything of an hour.

Lady Stuart was a very clever woman, but
all her cleverness seemed to be paralyzed before this unknown man who suddenly confronted her.

The hesitation which troubled her had not
otherwise brought about any apparent change
in her behavior in the regularity of her attention to the world, and she had again appeared
at the Tuileries since her presentation, either
in the ordinary circle of the ladies of the court
or at the regular Mondays of the Empress.

Napoleon III. had continued his good offices,
and nothing in the studied reserve which he
manifested in her presence seemed likely to
terminate her suspense, when one afternoon

when she was at home musing, and perhaps *ennuyée*, she was informed that a person who refused to give his name desired to speak with her.

For a moment, Lady Stuart thought of refusing to see this person who interfered with her reflections and her repose: but she was morose and nervous: she only saw in the visitor a welcome relief offered by chance to the sadness of her thoughts, and she ordered him to be admitted.

The man who then presented himself before her looked somewhat like a magistrate. Somewhat vulgar in features although irreproachably dressed, a red ribbon in the button-hole of his *redingote*, a smiling and inquisitive eye, as though moved by machinery or instinctive habit, he advanced towards the young lady and bowing profoundly, announced himself, as M. Hyrvoix.

When she heard the dreaded name of the chief of the Emperor's secret police, Lady Stuart involuntarily trembled, a fact which did not escape the cunning official and which evidently amused him, for a malicious smile curled his lip. The uneasiness of the Countess Ellen was easily accounted for. Having made a sensation at court she might fear anything, henceforth as she might in like manner hope for anything. She might fear that her beauty had given umbrage to the Empress, that her triumph had displeased some influential person, that her position even as a stranger—a somewhat mysterious stranger, playing almost the rôle of an adventuress, might have been suspected, and that for one of these reasons or even for all the reasons, M. Hyrvoix might have paid her this visit, with a courteous order for her to leave Paris.

The police officer read her apprehension and quickly dissipated it.

"Reassure yourself, madam," said he, "in spite of my name, and my functions, I am to-day a messenger of peace, and I am not here to cause any trouble in your house."

"Then, sir, you are welcome," replied the young woman, and assuming an air of frankness, she added, "kindly let me know the reason for your presence here."

Before giving this explanation and seating

himself, M. Hyrvoix cast a rapid glance around the room in which he was. It was a small room hung on all sides with tapestry.

"I ask your pardon madam, for delaying our conversation," said he, "but since that which I have to communicate to you is of a very delicate nature, and must be kept secret, I wish to be assured that there shall be no indiscreet listeners."

Lady Stuart, very much puzzled, rose, went out of the room and came in again, almost immediately, and locked the doors.

"I have given orders," she said, "that I am not to be disturbed under any pretext, and we have nothing to fear, as we are shut up here like two lovers."

M. Hyrvoix with a comical and at the same time a respectful gesture, disclaiming any sentimental feelings, drew near to the young lady in order to avoid the necessity of raising his voice, and confided to her the mission with which he had been entrusted.

"His Majesty, the Emperor, has sent me to you, madam," he began.

Lady Stuart in spite of herself, started, and her eyes flashed. " His Majesty ? "

" Yes, madam," rejoined the police official, who still remarked the nervousness of his interlocutor. "His Majesty has deigned to command me to inform you that he is very much interested in you, and that he would very much like to have an interview with you."

And very adroitly, pretending to have no doubt of the motives which actuated the Emperor, he added :

" You are a member, madam, of the highest circle of English society. During your residence in London, you have made the acquaintance of a great many political personages. I believe that his Majesty desires to obtain from you some confidential information which would be useful to him, and that would not involve you in any act prejudicing the interests of your country."

Lady Stuart was not the dupe of this ruse, or of the perfect correctness of the language, softening the extreme delicacy of the message which was sent to her. But following the example of M. Hyrvoix, she became an actress:

"I am at the Emperor's orders, sir," she declared, "and will wait until he deigns to interrogate me."

The police official continued:

"His Majesty desires, madam, that the interview which you are kind enough to grant him should take place outside of the Tuileries; would you object to the Emperor paying you a visit to-morrow evening, in the most absolute incognito?"

Matters were coming to a sudden crisis and Lady Stuart became a little pale.

"I repeat to you, sir, that I am ready to obey the orders of the Emperor. To-morrow I will give my servants a holiday and will be alone: he can come without fear of being compromised."

As she said this, she bowed, but of a sudden she recovered herself, and appeared to be alarmed.

"Do you know, sir, that this visit of the Emperor makes me very uneasy. If in spite of all precautions he should be recognized entering my house or leaving it; if some misfortune or accident, I know not what, should befall him, or threaten him; I am afraid, I confess, of the responsibility which I should incur in such an event. Do you not think that his Majesty would be imprudent to take such a step?"

M. Hyrvoix made a gesture of indifference with his hand.

"Have no fear, madam, for the safety of the Emperor. I shall be with his Majesty and know how to take care of him."

Lady Stuart smiled softly.

"You are indeed, a devoted servant," she said.

M. Hyrvoix who had risen and was about to leave the room, replied mockingly:

"You will see, madam." He then left the young lady.

When a servant came to announce to Lady Stuart that dinner was served, he found her stretched on the cushions in the same little room in which she had received M. Hyrvoix, and it was automatically that she went to the dining-room, with her thoughts far away from her surroundings. She was alone. She touched none of the dishes offered to her; she ordered champagne, drank two or three glasses and abruptly leaving the table, ran and locked herself in her room, where, her nerves all unstrung, she threw herself on her bed and sobbed. The joys and sorrows of life have this singularity in common, that we often shed tears when approaching them. Was this a joy or a sorrow which confronted Lady Stuart? She could not have answered this question; but she paid her tribute to the mysterious future by weeping.

CHAPTER VI.

WHEN the Emperor made his appearance the next day at the appointed hour, at the young lady's house, she was calm: she had a very well-defined idea of the long-wished for results which would be the consequence of this meeting. Ready to yield, she had resolved to place a price upon the surrender of her virtue, and it was with the most perfect confidence in a lasting *liaison* that she awaited her imperial visitor.

What she had to fear was that the Emperor might, as he had done with other women, having accomplished his purpose, forget her. As soon, in fact, as he was seated beside her, Napoleon was tender and passionate, and gave her to understand without much circumlocution or oratorical effects, the feelings he entertained for her.

Thus commenced, the interview could have but one result: a surrender which would be forgotten as soon as granted.

Lady Stuart was well aware that if she trifled too long with the sovereign, in this excessively refined manner, that her projects would fail; that her hopes would share the same fate as those of the others who had enjoyed the imperial intimacy for a brief period and had been deceived.

With a studied reserve and an amiable coquetry, and ever on her guard she allowed the Emperor to address her: she listened to the avowal of his love as well as of his overmastering passion; but when he attempted to become bolder, she defended herself and with a clever finesse, again became mistress of the situation.

Half laughing, half angry, she checked the ardor of her visitor:

"Are you really sincere, sire," she said, "and are you not deceiving me and yourself, as to the importance and the real nature of the sentiments which you entertain for me?"

The Emperor a little taken aback, stammered: "I assure you madam. . . . . ."

"Yes, yes," replied Lady Stuart, "I know, I guess all that you are going to say to me—all that you have doubtless said to so many other women. It is just that that I do not wish to hear. I am not to be wooed like all women, or rather I do not respond in the same manner as they do to the tender speeches which are addressed to me."

Napoleon III. who was more and more surprised and even vexed at the attitude of the young lady—an attitude for which he had been but ill prepared—tried to speak again, but she did not allow him to recover himself.

"I am explaining myself," she continued; "certainly, sire, I do not ignore the value of your affection. But I am also aware that if it brings a great and fleeting joy to some women it also is the cause to others less numerous, more sensitive and more solicitous for themselves,—of griefs and regrets which are not ephemeral. You say you love me. I will not affect to conceal my feelings— it will be easy for me to meet your avowal by an identical confession. But in this community of ideas and sentiments which draws us together, lurks exactly the danger which menances us, the danger which I wish to avoid.—You are inconstant, sire; you have not even the strength to be faithful to one woman. You would be faithless to me if I yielded to your prayers, as you have been with others. You would perhaps forget me quicker than you have all the other women, because I surrendered more quickly, even though you have not forgotten those that you have fascinated. And if the moments which had been ours should fade from your memory, it would be grievous to my heart and my pride. Is it not better considering the inequality of feelings and position existing between us, that I should remain as far as a more intimate relation is concerned, a stranger."

The Emperor was not accustomed to meet with so eloquent a resistance, from the women whom he honored with his notice at the Court. He realized that he had to deal with an uncommon individuality, and in place of growing weary of listening to her, so far from being repulsed by this half refusal, it only inflamed his passion.

Lady Stuart seemed to desire a decisive declaration, a promise which it would be impossible for him to evade. He made no attempt to avoid this explanation, and in the words which he uttered and which are very curious, he made her the promise which she desired without having dared to formulate it.

Rising from his seat and walking up and down the room with his hands behind his back, he began to talk at first hurriedly, then more slowly and deliberately, and soon the sound of his voice which at first was harsh, became softer and, as it were, rhythmical.

" You are right, madam," he said, "you are not one of those women whom one abandons, and who serve for the satisfaction of a fleeting caprice. You are as clever as you are beautiful, and you deserve to be truly loved, and to inspire a lasting passion. It is thus that I desire to love you, and you are wrong in taunting me with the inconstancy which I have shown— I do not deny it, on former occasions. Ah, this inconstancy with which I am reproached, if you knew the causes of it, if those even who have suffered from it, could have guessed the motives for it, it would not appear to you, it would no longer appear to them, as blameworthy. A man can say many things, madam, to a woman, especially to a woman whom he desires to be his; and I am going, if you will allow me, to make a confession. I am inconstant, I seek and desire the caresses of woman: but why am I thus, why is there in me this ardent love of pleasure, never satiated, ever reviving? It is a painful confession to make; but you will believe it for you are the only woman who has ever spoken to me as you have done. I haved loved, madam, profoundly, foolishly, and I was deceived. I staked my political fortune, my name, the prestige of my throne, the devotion of my partisans, against the heart of a woman, and in exchange for all these sacrifices, my reward was indifference. This is the secret of what is called my inconstancy, and my numerous *bonnes fortunes.*"

Lady Stuart who had been listening to the Emperor with interest and almost with terror, moved abruptly and an involuntary cry burst from her lips:

" How, sire, the Empress. . . !"

Napoleon III, turned to her and stopping in his walk up and down the room, said somewhat harshly:

" The Empress does not love me, madam, the Empress has never loved me. My case is common I know, and I am not the only man whom fate treats thus. My fellow-sufferers generally seek relief for their bitter sorrow in drinking or gambling. A sovereign can neither drink nor gamble, but there remains for him the fair sex. I flew to it, in the same way as the unhappy lover or husband has recourse to absinthe or the card-table. You see that my inconstancy is easily accounted for and that there is nothing in it that a woman who is sincerely loved as I feel that I love you, need fear or for which she has a right to reproach me."

The Emperor grew silent. Then he resumed his pacing up and down the room, doubtless waiting for Lady Stuart to recall him to her side. But the young lady leaning her elbow on a divan, was lost in thought, and her half-closed eyes seemed to be fixed upon a disquieting vision.

Napoleon III. broke the profound silence:

"You do not answer me, madam," he said.

Lady Stuart looked at him languidly.

"What shall I say to you, sire," she murmured. "The confidence you have reposed in me, disquiets me and gives me pleasure at the same time. . . ."

And as the Emperor advanced towards her

she bowed, and added, keeping him at a distance with outstretched arm:

"I pity you and I love you."

Napoleon III. attempted to possess himself of the hand which was lightly touching him. But Lady Stuart softly repulsed him, and said pleadingly:

"Yes, I love you sire, but that confession does not mean that I am yours. I should certainly be happy, nay proud to afford you some happiness, to heal the wounds in your soul. But this is too high an honor for me and I dare not hope for it. I pray you, retire and leave me: I must reflect and ask myself, whether in giving myself to you, in becoming your mistress— why should I shirk the word?—I shall be able to afford you the consolation you deserve: for henceforth your happiness will be my only care."

And she repeated:

"I beg you leave me—I wish to be alone."

The Emperor in the satisfaction which he felt in the thought that this woman would be his, that she morally belonged to him already even though his bliss was deferred for a time, remained silent. The scene that Lady Stuart had brought about made him timid, and he stammered like a bashful youth as he imploringly said:

"How am I to see you again, madam, and learn your decision?"

The young woman allayed his uneasiness.

"The next time that I go to the Tuileries, I will give you an answer, sire. If I wear no jewels, you may consider me your most faithful friend."

The Emperor had wished to obtain a more formal promise, but he understood that Lady Stuart would grant him nothing more at this first private interview than an enigmatical assurance; and when he left her with the half certainty, which she had given him, he felt that the Countess Ellen had inspired him with an undying passion.

However, the young woman, as she saw him leave her, was satisfied with herself, and the ability with which she had inflamed his passion, and of the positive assurances he had

5

given her as to the nature and consequences of her future *liaison*.

Lady Stuart had not deceived herself, in truth, regarding the feelings and impressions which she had excited in the breast of him who reigned at the Tuileries. He awaited her coming to the Château with feverish impatience; and when she made her appearance a few days after the conversation which has just been related, he experienced a delicious thrill of delight.

CHAPTER VII.

THE year 1866 ended with all Europe, nay, the world anticipating eagerly, the grand spectacle of the Exposition which the Empire had provided, and the opening of the Exposition was the signal for the redoubling of the fêtes and follies at the Court.

The Emperors and Kings who visited the Tuileries in those days were dazzled and even somewhat frightened. These men and these women who presented themselves before them in all the incontestable charm of elegant frivolities, surprised them; and while they enjoyed the seductive society of these agreeable beings, they could not refrain from thinking that the courtiers of Napoleon III. were on the road to ruin. The Court appeared to the stranger like a reunion of males and females created for pleasure, with no thought but the enjoyment of the hour, and carried away by their passions.

Men, no matter what their social condition —kings or citizens—are not puritans, and are not obstinate defenders of virtue, except when among themselves and under their own roof, they have special and personal reasons for appearing severe.

The rulers of States, whom Napoleon III. invited to his Court in 1867, rapidly recovered from the astonishment that they had felt at first at the attitude of the frequenters of the Tuileries, and as, after all, they had not come to Paris to be bored, they eagerly accepted the entertainments given in their honor, and not disdaining even to join in them as actors, they amused themselves.

When the Exposition was opened Lady Stuart had already for some time been the mistress of the Emperor.

She succeeded at the Court of the sovereign, to a woman to whom he had long been devoted. This woman—whom it is not necessary to name here—had herself taken the place of the famous Comtesse de Castiglione, in the affections of the Emperor, and, to a greater extent than she, had been his political adviser. Very beautiful, she was still more remarkable for her talents, and notwithstanding certain incidents she had succeeded in attaching herself to Napoleon, while at the same time she was one of the inseparable friends of the Empress. In addition to this the sovereign had need of her services more in an intellectual than a sensual capacity, and he had not hesitated to exert his authority openly to protect her against all attacks. Lady Stuart certainly could not have competed with her in the knowledge of politics. She did not attempt to do so, and wisely contented herself with the offering of her caresses, permitting the Emperor to continue the worldly and business relations with her rival which it would have been almost impossible for him to sever.

The Exposition, in engrossing the time and attention of Napoleon III., and thereby placing an enforced reserve on his *liaison* with Lady Stuart, by causing interruptions in his intimacy with her, had made of the young woman a mistress, who appreciated to the full her influence over him she loves, still she had never been able definitely to assert this power.

In fact it was not until the close of the imperial fêtes that she exerted the full force of her fascinations.

Napoleon III. had certainly passed pleasant hours in the company of women,—with Mme. de Castiglione, and with the person of whom I incidentally spoke above,—and towards the end of his reign with the Comtesse d'Argenteau, whose opinions and talents he also valued. But it may be affirmed without fear of contradiction, that he never was so happy with any of them as with Lady Stuart.

This pleasure arose not only from the physical beauty of this woman, but from the manner in which this sensual beauty affected him. With all the other women,—especially those whom I have just designated—for I do not count the ephemeral *amours* which a fleeting caprice cast into the arms of the sovereign—the passionate nature of the Emperor was always dominated by the habitual exchange of opinions on the political questions of the day, and it was in consequence of this peculiar condition which characterized his *liaisons*, that there was a sort of coldness or constraint, which fatally weakened his ardor.

A woman, no matter how beautiful she may be, will never be the absolute mistress of her lover, if she seeks to impose on that lover a moral as well as a physical influence. A man will love such a woman, will unite his life with hers, will be unhappy if he is separated from her, but his joy or his sorrow will be rather the result of his intellectual than his physical feelings –for his mind alone will be in sympathy with the mind of the woman, his love for her will be absolutely free from sensuality. A man may love such a woman, I repeat, but he will never have the feeling for her that he would experience for a woman who is loved on account only of her physical attractions, that emotion excited by the human animal, if you will, who without speech or thought, magnetically attracts the male by the pure strength of her superb animality—as the flower in full bloom, rich with subtle perfumes allures greedy insects with its juicy sap.

Great voluptuaries do not insist upon a woman being clever. They only exact that she shall have the power to excite love.

The Emperor was a great voluptuary, and as Lady Stuart did not trouble the relations which he had with her, by any preoccupation foreign to the passion with which she inspired him, he found with her, more than with all her predecessors in his affections, the sweetness and the fervor which constitute a real passion.

Only one woman, Margaret Bellengé, had

ever been able to absorb the love of Napoleon III., in a like degree with Lady Stuart. Margaret Bellengé, resorted to no other art than the power of her caresses to enslave the Emperor, and it was in this that lay her power in her *liaison* with him.

When the great excitement on account of the Exposition had subsided at the Tuileries, the Emperor turned with renewed ardor to the society of his mistress. He met her frequently and passed many happy hours with her.

It was now a year since Lady Stuart had been presented at Court, and it must be acknowleged that in that time she had made rapid and triumphant progress.

Her influence over Napoleon was so great that she scarcely took the trouble to dissimulate, and even took a malicious pleasure in letting it be seen when she appeared at the Château, to which she was regularly invited.

The position which she occupied in the heart of the Emperor, could not continue to be ignored at the Palace under these conditions, and in fact soon her *liaison* with the Emperor was the topic of all the gossips, and with a thousand details, true or false, went the rounds among the *habitués* of the Château.

The Empress who always was well-informed on matters of this kind, heard of the Countess Ellen's intrigue, and was much irritated. She determined to put a stop to the scandal of which her house was the theatre.

The Empress knew all the mistresses of Napoleon III. At first when she heard of an intrigue of the Emperor she used to pout, become nervous and even rude in her manner. But she soon seemed to become accustomed to the vagaries of her husband, and she tolerated with an appearance of indifference the presence of the woman who became her rival. She simply avenged herself on the Emperor for his infidelities by upbraidings and anger.

The same thing would have taken place without doubt in regard to Lady Stuart, if an event had not occurred which made the situation still more serious.

CHAPTER VIII.

ALL of a sudden the Countess Ellen ceased her visits to the Tuileries, abruptly left Paris and no one could say at first where she had gone.

But this sudden flight excited curiosity, and many comments. The Empress herself was astonished at an absence which nothing seemed to justify. At last some of the more curious who had been into the country in search of the Countess, declared on their return that Lady Stuart, who was *enceinte* by the Emperor, had taken refuge in a village near Paris, to await her confinement.

This was true. Lady Stuart, dismayed and happy at one and the same time, had informed her imperial lover one afternoon, that she was about to become a mother.

The Emperor was well aware of the apprehension that the Empress felt on the score of his *amours* and their probable consequences. He knew that it would not do for his companion to aver that her child owed its existence to him, and to publish the fact to the world. He knew that in her exultation she might be capable of even worse imprudences, and foreseeing almost with a feeling of terror, the results of such a revelation, he insisted on the immediate departure of his mistress.

The scene in which Lady Stuart informed Napoleon III. of her approaching maternity was not without its simple charm and at the same time its emotional features.

When the astonished Emperor remained for some minutes without making any reply to the young lady, she became uneasy.

"Ah, sire," said she, "love me well to-day, for to-morrow without doubt, we shall be as much strangers to one another as if we had never met."

Napoleon III. looked at her steadily:

"Why do you talk thus?" he asked.

"Because, in confessing to you that I am about to be a mother, sire, I feel that the word '*fini*' is written on the last page of our romance."

"You are mistaken. I love you sufficiently, madam, to make it impossible for me to forget you, or give you up, even should some sad accident happen to put a stop to our relations. You are about to become a mother and I do not conceal from you that I should have preferred that this were not to be. But it is not so much this statement that worries me. I think of the child that is about to come into the world, who is mine as much as yours, and whom I shall not be able to love."

Lady Stuart trembled.

"What, sire, you will not love my child, our child?" she anxiously asked.

"Alas, madam, there are difficult situations in life. Understand me. Do not private citizens, the *bourgeois*, gentlemen, frequently affect to ignore in obedience to the laws and social usages, a son or a daughter, the offspring of a loved mistress? These laws and these usages, which are binding on citizens, are much more binding on kings and public men. I am

sad because I shall not be able to love your
child as I should have liked to love him, because
I think of all those who are in the same situation and who less fortunate for your child
will be fortunate—sorrowfully wander about
the world. Love has its cruelties and a paternity that cannot be acknowledged as one among
them."

The Emperor was born with kindly and
paternal instincts. He fondly loved his legitimate son, the Prince Imperial; and would
have liked to love as dearly and openly, perhaps, the illegitimate child with whose destiny
he was charged.

Lady Stuart was touched by the kindness of
his words, and the tenderly melancholy philosophy, he evinced, and she made no objection,
when he pointed out to her that she must leave
Paris at once.

After having made arrangements for a prolonged absence, she went to Versailles under a
feigned name and there awaited the birth of
her child.

The Emperor was sincerely vexed when he

saw that his intimate friends and the Empress had discovered the cause of the absence of his mistress, and heard the remarks that were provoked by the disappearance of the young woman. He would very much have liked to put a stop to these scandals which it must be acknowledged were now no longer scandals, but he could not without compromising his dignity, notice the reports in circulation among the courtiers, by denying the truth of them or to censure their impropriety. Would they have paid any attention to his intervention or even obeyed him? One may well doubt the efficacy of this intervention, when it is remembered that the Empress was always omnipotent at the Tuileries, and that the frequenters of the Château took their tone from her, and that the Court circle, both men and women, would have made light of the displeasure of Napoleon III., in order the better to please her whose despotic authority they acknowledged.

However, one day at one of the Empress' Mondays, the Emperor lost patience and gave the scandal-mongers a lecture.

As he passed near a group of ladies who were joking with a number of young men, he heard the name of Lady Stuart mentioned, and that these whisperings seemed to involve some mystery connected with this name.

He was only too well aware of the nature of this conversation and walked straight up to the speakers.

As he approached, all were silent, and bowed uneasily in the hope that he would proceed: but the Emperor stopped and slowly stroking his mustache, he uttered these words;

" I invite you ladies, and you also gentlemen, to be present at the next sermon to be preached in the chapel of the Château: the text will be on evil speaking and our duty to our neighbor."

And he added as he turned his back on them:

" I may count, may I not, on your presence?"

The amazed courtiers dispersed. The incident made some noise at Court, and from this time forth, in spite of their submission to the Empress, the courtiers were more prudent in their gossip.

But the scandal which the authority of the Emperor had put a stop to for a time, broke out without restriction at Court, when it was known that Lady Stuart had given birth to a son.

The young lady thought that she had arranged everything around her so that her secret should not be revealed, and even that her *accouchement* should not be known. But she had acted without taking into consideration the thousand traitresses who menace even the humblest and who watched her all the more closely because she was powerful and envied.

As soon as possible after its birth, the infant was entrusted to a woman, carefully selected: of good-natured appearance, a sort of cityfied peasant, who lived at a small place near Rambouillet, and who carried off her nursling even before the mother had recovered from the shock of her illness.

After her son was taken away Lady Stuart was very sad. This tardy and somewhat irregular advent of a child, too forcibly reminded her of the years when as a married woman she had prayed for a maternity which had ever been denied to her, for her not to feel deeply the cruel separation from the little creature she had brought into the world. It would have been so sweet for her to have been able to keep him with her to talk to him and receive his innocent caresses, and in the bitterness of her sorrow she began to hate the vanities which engrossed her life and everything which she had desired, and which she would have gladly exchanged for one hour of real independence.

But she knew that this independence was a dream which could not be realized in the existence which she had accepted: and as the Emperor loved her and was impatiently awaiting her, she resigned herself to the inevitable and resolved to leave Versailles as soon as her health should be re-established.

As soon as she was able to go out her first thought was not for her lover, but for her son alone.

She went to La Verrière, where they had taken her child, and spent the whole day with him, happy in looking at him, kissing him, giving herself up to the charming foolishness of mothers—which is also sad—who when deprived of their children, seem to wish to devour them when they are permitted to visit them.

This was in the month of August, 1868. The house where the little boy had been placed stood in the middle of a tolerably large garden, and Lady Stuart, delighted at playing the part of mamma, had withdrawn under the shade of some trees with her son.

All of a sudden, as she was tossing him on her knees, and trying to coax a laugh to his lips, that first laugh so dear to all mothers, she remarked that her son had a scar behind his right ear. She was alarmed until she discovered after a careful examination, that what she had taken for a wound was only a birth-mark. In fact, the child had on the edge of his ear a red pimple, which stood out in relief on his white skin, like a large pea.

Reassured, she pressed her lips to the "beauty spot," and having returned the baby to his nurse, went away.

Some time after her visit to her son, she returned to society and this return was a memorable one.

As the Court was out of town for the summer months, she did not make her appearance there. This was by advice of the Emperor, who thought it better to postpone her advent among his intimate friends for the present; but he resumed his interrupted intimacy with her, and she visited him more than once, unknown to those who believed that her maternity would cause a rupture between her and the Emperor.

However, Lady Stuart was not unaware of the remarks of which she had been the object during her long absence, the slanders and calumnies which had been levelled against her by the frequenters of the Château, and she was in a hurry, in a spirit of bravado and reprisal, to show herself to those men— who had so pitilessly persecuted her with their sarcasms,— more beautiful perhaps, more powerful and more envied than before the event which had caused her exile from Paris.

CHAPTER IX.

It was again a fête given at the Tuileries, in the winter of 1868, which served Lady Stuart for a pretext to return to Court.

The Emperor who feared a scandal tried to dissuade her from taking this foolish step, and advised her to make her return to the Tuileries in a less ostentatious manner, but she refused to listen to him, and revolted against the ostracism under which she was suffering, and with a caress, she obtained the consent of the sovereign.

The Emperor's fears notwithstanding were not unfounded, and Lady Stuart with all her audacity recoiled on this occasion before the anger and the superlatively contemptuous attitude of the Empress.

When the Countess Ellen entered the *salons* leaning on the arm of Comte d'A., one of the Chamberlains specially deputed by Napoleon

III. to escort the young lady, there was a manifestation which left no doubt as to the feelings and impressions which her presence inspired.

There arose around her a low murmur, and while some looked at her with anxious curiosity, and with a sort of stupefaction, others pretended not to see her, not willing to compromise themselves with the Empress by saluting her, or to displease the Emperor, by being too ostentatiously sparing in their homage.

Lady Stuart, without appearing to remark this defection and this hypocrisy, had by this time reached the *salon* where the Empress was and advancing towards her she prepared to give the customary curtsy. Then there was a dramatic scene, and all around anxiously awaited the result.

The Empress when she saw Lady Stuart, sprang up from her seat as though impelled by a spring, drew herself up to her full height and looked at her rival, her face pale, haughty and severe and her hands trembling.

Her attendants were silent and seemed panic-stricken.

Without being disconcerted by the reception of the sovereign Lady Stuart advanced a little nearer, and as nothing unusual took place she bowed and smiled.

But the Empress remained motionless acknowledging neither her salute nor her smile; and when the Countess Ellen rose, she saw her in the same posture, hostile, angry and reproachful.

Then she understood that it was impossible for her to appear thenceforth at the Tuileries, and that she must leave the Palace where she had formerly triumphed.

Erect in her turn, with a frowning countenance, and flashing eyes, she met the attitude of the Empress with one equally defiant.

A moment—at most a few seconds—the two women stood thus, threateningly facing one another, asking themselves perhaps, whether if forgetful of their rank and the place where they were, they should not like common women, fly at each other, like animals meeting with the desire of gratifying the instinct of revenge.

In truth it is impossible to say how this scene

would have ended, if the Emperor, who had not
lost a single detail, had not come to the rescue.
He sent Comte d'A. to Lady Stuart, and the
Chamberlain again offering his arm to the insulted favorite, drew her away, veiling his authoritative interference by a flattering remark.

Countess Ellen who did not easily lose her
self-possession when she saw that a quarrel with
the Empress would irretrievably ruin her, as
far as her intimacy with her lover was concerned, followed M. d'A. apparently without
reluctance.

But as she was unwilling to acknowledge her
defeat, she said to him, laying a stress upon the
words:

"Is it for the purpose of taking me to my
carriage, sir, that you show me so much politeness?"

M. d'A., who felt a little embarrassed at the
duty which had been imposed on him that
night, replied:

"I have received no order on the subject,
madam. I am simply instructed by the Emperor, to beg of you to avoid the *salon* of the

Empress and I dare respectfully to counsel you to abide by this advice."

He then left the young lady.

Prince Napoleon, who had observed all the phases of the little drama that had just taken place, happened to be at the moment near Lady Stuart.

He approached her and held a long conversation with her and the news of this conversation, which caused a great deal of comment at first, when it reached the Empress, had no small share in increasing the hatred which the Empress felt for her cousin.

On this occasion, however, the Empress was wrong to be angry with him. This evening the Prince only stopped to compliment the Countess Ellen on her beauty, and as he was a charming and gallant man he succeeded in interesting her.

Nevertheless the young lady affected to consider the chat which she had with the Prince as a compensation for her reception by the sovereign and retired without having spoken to any of the other guests.

The reserve of the Emperor who had designedly kept aloof from her, during the short time that she was at the Château, caused her much pain and uneasiness. Although this reserve was perfectly natural under the circumstances, and was easily accounted for, the Countess Ellen was resolved not to accept it, and to know if it did not menace some danger to her or her *liaison*.

The day after this memorable evening, she wrote to the Emperor soliciting an interview.

Napoleon III. came to see her, and as apart from the affectionate reproaches he addressed to her relative to her foolish freak and the lamentable consequences which might result from it,—he was as prodigal of his caresses as before the incident,—she was appeased. Even her hatred for the Empress assumed a platonic form which was not without spirit. She was forbidden the Tuileries henceforth, but in spite of the affront which she had received and which she was powerless to resent, was she not the more powerful, since she was mistress of the heart and affections of the man who was master at the Palace?

In the whirl of gaiety at the Tuileries and the Embassies during the winter season of 1868, in the vortex of their pleasures, the appearance and the absence of Lady Stuart were quickly forgotten in the Emperor's circle.

The Empress equally devoted to her pleasures seemed to have entirely forgotten the existence of her rival, and of the somewhat dramatic scene which had caused her withdrawal from the Court. As she did not refer to the matter, and pretended to have forgotten that a woman one evening had dared to defy her in her Palace, no one cared to recall this woman and her action towards the sovereign.

However, the forgetfulness and tranquillity of the Empress were all on the surface, as, owing to her ardent, impressionable nature she was unable quickly to forget a face and an action which had so cruelly wounded her feelings, and had seemed to endanger for the moment not her affection for the Emperor—for she no longer loved her husband,—but her position and the right of being servilely obeyed as a queen,—and of seeing the slightest as well as the most extravagant of her caprices gratified.

In truth, the Empress thought of Lady Stuart and above all of the child, which was the fruit of the young lady's relations with the Emperor, and its existence rather than the strong passion with which the Countess Ellen had inspired Napoleon III., irritated her.

At certain times, the image of this child presented itself to her as a living irony hostiled to her own maternity, as a menace liable to spring up at some indefinite period, in the already uncertain future of her own son, and the future of the imperial dynasty, endangered at this time by violent political feelings, and the ceaseless clamors of a hostile opposition, determined on its overthrow.

The Empress had never really loved her husband, neither did she love her son. In marrying the Emperor she had but one end in view, to rule, to be the absolute mistress of both the man and the people, to exchange the life of an adventuress and a foreign name, for the illustrious one of Bonaparte,—for the possession of a throne, for the proud existence and all the worldly happiness of a queen. The Empress had the soul and the callous feelings of an ambitious courtesan. She was immensely vain, with an overmastering greed for pleasure and wealth. These were the passions that actuated her in the wonderful and cleverly conducted plot which ended in her marriage, and made her without a peer in the art of seduction. In endeavoring to protect her son against any ambiguous or irregular paternity, in pitilessly pursuing with her implacable enmity any bastard offspring of the Emperor, the same vanity, the same desire for personal satisfaction, and not the sincere solicitude and the fond love which mothers lavish on their children, animated her. She avoided impending dangers, by protecting her son from them, and if she could have been assured that an illegitimate brother of the Prince Imperial would not have endangered her plans for the future, either politically or in her family relations, she would not have hesitated for the sake of her own peace of mind to banish from her life the anxieties with which she was beset in the present uncertainty.

CHAPTER X.

The Empress knew well how to conceal the anxiety which the birth of the son of Lady Stuart caused her, during the month succeeding the incident which signalized the last appearance of the young lady at the Tuileries. But soon this anxiety under the influence of the thought which troubled her, became evident and it was almost in spite of herself that she allowed it to be surmised.

One afternoon when she was chatting with some of her intimate friends, among whom was the Princess Pauline de Metternich, she suddenly broke off the conversation and made the startling remark : —

"Nobody here talks about that Englishwoman any more, who endeavored to revolutionize the Tuileries—that Lady Stuart. Which of you ladies can tell me what has become of this woman?"

There was a silence—a long silence.

But as the Empress manifested impatience for an answer to her question, one of the ladies present, Mme. P. mustered up courage to reply.

"The Empress is really too good to remember the adventuress; Lady Stuart, I am told, is living a very retired life, no doubt from regret at having displeased your Majesty."

The Empress not satisfied with this vague explanation, rejoined :—

"She has a child, a son, whose father is unknown, hasn't she, for whom she desires to claim the Emperor as father? I am more interested in the child than in her. What has she done with it? where is it?"

This time it was the Comtesse de M. who replied :—

"It appears she has got rid of it. The child is at nurse, at a distance from Paris, and the claims which Lady Stuart endeavors to make on his behalf are too ridiculous even to be listened to."

The sovereign turned to Mme. de M.

" I don't agree with you," she said, and her usually harsh voice became even harsher; "claims of this kind, however foolish, always find more fools than enough to listen to them and believe in them."

The Princess de Metternich, who, up to this point, had not taken any part in the conversation, advanced :—

" In my country," she declared, "such stories as these would not trouble the heart or the mind of those at whom they are aimed, we should simply and without any fuss suppress the cause of the scandal and that would end all."

This woman—the Princess de Metternich—this red-haired Austrian, coolly counselled the commission of a crime, as coolly indeed as she would have advised an excursion to the country. Although the frivolous and unscrupulous women who were listening to her had not many scruples, they understood her suggestion, and with instinctive feminine pity, they shuddered, awaiting the reply of the Empress in painful suspense.

The sovereign did not shudder at the abominable words of Mme. de Metternich.

A cold smile curled her lips, and she murmured the same speech that she had made when it was claimed that Marie Bellengé owed her maternity to the Emperor:—

"I will never allow a bastard true or false to be brought up in view of the Prince Imperial. You may be sure that I shall use every means in my power to save my son annoyance."

In expressing herself thus the Empress evidently had just formulated a design against the innocent little child of whom they were speaking, and as they knew her to be capable of still worse resolutions when her obstinate brain entertained a fixed idea, the ladies surrounding her were alarmed at the harshness of her words.

The same apprehension seized them all: the Empress had determined that the son of Lady Stuart should disappear. What would be the actual consequences and nature of this condemnation?

If this conversation had been continued, the Empress might perhaps have been induced to satisfy the anxious curiosity of her intimate friends. But she dropped the subject and assuming a merry air with as much ease as she had been grave, she apparently dismissed the subject from her thoughts.

A startling event happened a few weeks after the utterance of these threats, which increased the irritation of the Empress.

After the scene which took place at the Tuileries between her and Lady Stuart, the sovereign was willing to believe and had even imagined that the Emperor from a feeling of personal prudence, as well as out of consideration for the dignity of his household, would have dropped his relations with his mistress.

As she had no information on this point, she made enquiries, having instructed one of her intimate friends to keep a watch on the Emperor, and it was not long before she learned that not only had Napoleon III. not broken off his intimacy with the Countess Ellen, but that he saw her oftener and more unrestrainedly, than when she appeared at Court.

She flew into a violent passion then and realizing that the tenacity of the Emperor's passion was due to the existence of the child on whom he doted—she decided to bring about a separation between Lady Stuart and her lover, an irretrievable separation from one who appeared to retain his affections by her caresses more than all the women who had preceded her.

As the reproaches with which she had already loaded the Emperor on account of his *liaison*, had not the slightest effect, she never thought of renewing them, and realized that if she wished to succeed in her undertaking, she must henceforth resort to more practical measures.

These measures presented themselves. In order to bring about a rupture between Napoleon III. and Lady Stuart, it became necessary not to overwhelm the sovereign with more or less efficacious reproaches and to the point, but to strike without pity at the woman who infatuated him.

This woman in herself, on account of her nationality, and her social rank, was beyond all attack or direct quarrel, and was beyond the reach of an arbitrary attack which would not be sanctioned by the Emperor's authority.

The perfidious and insinuating words of Mme. de Metternich, rang in the ears of the Empress, and the more she recalled them, the more was she persuaded that they indicated the only way of carrying out her design.

Once the Englishwoman's child was out of the way or at least had disappeared, a crisis would arise between the two lovers which would put an end to their tranquil affection and terminate the intimacy which united them. The same effort and the same bold stroke would restore to the Emperor his moral independence and deliver the Prince Imperial from a future and probable evil.

The Empress carefully matured her plans and when her resolution was fixed in her mind, she took measures to put it in execution.

Whilst the sovereign was thus plotting against her, Lady Stuart was ignorant of the dangers which threatened her, and was happy in the enjoyment of the love which the Emperor continued to lavish on her and above all was she proud of the secret influence which on account of this love she exercised at the Tuileries.

Her tranquillity was destined to be tragically interrupted. The young woman went nearly every month to La Verrière to see her son. It was then the beginning of the year 1869 and the child was about six months old with all the mischievous tricks and charming grace of a kitten, which rejoiced and amused his mother.

One afternoon about the end of January, when Lady Stuart reached the house of the good people who had charge of her child, she was surprised to find the house closed and almost abandoned.

An instinctive fear of some misfortune seized her, in presence of this solitude: but she was soon reassured by the brightness of the winter sun, and told herself that it was easy to explain the absence of the child's guardians, that they had doubtless taken advantage of the fine weather to take a walk, and that they would soon return.

In order that the time might not seem too long while she was waiting for them, she went into the village and entered the woods in the vicinity. When she returned the house was no longer empty, and she went in.

When they saw Lady Stuart, the man and his wife, who were accustomed to receive her with respect, rose from their seats and exchanged looks of astonishment.

The Countess Ellen without noticing this reception, saluted them politely, and as her custom was, followed her salutation by the question;—

"Well nurse, and how is Jack? Bring him to me quick."

These words were always followed by the appearance of the child and the young lady would carry him off and nearly devour him with her caresses.

But on this occasion when they heard these words the child's guardians were thunderstruck and overwhelmed with astonishment.

While they remained motionless and silent, Lady Stuart who had placed her cloak on a chair, and was arranging some little presents which she had brought, re-entered the room. Their embarrassment and astonishment now struck her suddenly. With a terrible presentiment, she bounded towards them.

"Didn't you hear me? go and fetch me my son."

The woman at last decided to speak.

"We heard you quite well, madam. . . ."

The Countess turned pale: "Well!" she said.

Instead of replying, the child's guardians moved uneasily.

"Well," said the young lady, "do as I tell you."

They murmured: "It happens that. . ."

Then Lady Stuart cried out:

"What is going on here . . . my son Jack, what have you done with him . . . I want to see him . . . I will . . ."

The words died away on her lips and as they made no reply to her imperious command, or to her anxious questions, she knew that something terrible had happened in this house since her last visit, and which was about to be revealed to her.

"Jack, Jack," she cried, "my child—my poor little one . . ."

Then turning to the affrighted guardians of her child, and expressing her fear in one sentence, she said:

"You miserable, miserable creatures, speak, speak then. What have you done with my child?"

The woman in presence of this grief broke down and sobbed bitterly.

The man who was calmer but livid, approached Lady Stuart and said to her:—

"We do not understand your visit to-day, madam, or your surprise and grief. Some fifteen days ago, a lady came here on your behalf, and carried off your child. This separation caused us much grief, for we loved the little one as if it had been our own. To console us for this sudden separation, the lady on your behalf, gave us a large sum of money. At first, we wished to refuse this gift, for it could not assauge our grief, but we are not rich and we ended by accepting it. We asked one another why, all of a sudden, without any motive, you took the child from us and why you sent a person whom we had never seen to fetch the child away, instead of coming here yourself. But we did not think it was our business to question your messenger, since she gave us no explanation of your resolution : and since you are a beautiful woman, madam, and no doubt very much occupied with your duties to society, we did not think it very strange that not having the time to come yourself, you should send another to do what you could not attend to yourself. This lady took the child away. Since it was taken away, we have had no news of it and can give you no news regarding it."

The man expressed himself simply and clearly, and Lady Stuart felt that he was telling truth!

She wailed : "*Mon Dieu, Mon Dieu*, they have stolen my child!"

Then addressing the guardians, she said :

"You have been deceived—they have lied to you. I never sent a lady to you to take away my little Jack."

As the woman was still weeping, the husband again spoke:

"The trick was well played in that case. But it will be easy for you, madam, to find out who has stolen your child. Those who have contrived this trick must be known to you and you must look among them for your child."

This argument was logical. Lady Stuart felt the strength of it, and a sort of light dawned upon her paralyzed perceptions.

Overwhelmed with grief but having somewhat recovered her sang-froid, she murmured :—

"Yes, certain people hate me and they are the ones who have committed this crime."

And she added with a discouraged gesture, as if replying to an inward suggestion:

"But shall I ever be able to reach them, shall I ever know what they have done with my poor little child?"

"Madam," said the man, "unhappily we are not in a position to be of service to you under the circumstances. I have told you all that we know of this affair. But do not despair. You know the names of those who wish you evil. Well, since you are rich, remember that with money you can have, and do, all that you wish: you will not be long before you recover your child from those who have stolen it."

Lady Stuart rose to leave. It was useless for her to remain any longer with these good people, and she was drawn to Paris by every fibre of her being, to him in whom she placed all her hope, to whom she would cry in her distress—the Emperor.

CHAPTER XI.

THE day after her sad discovery, she went to the Tuileries at the risk of meeting the Empress, and imperiously demanded an interview with Napoleon III.

The sovereign received her immediately, but when he saw her he made a gesture of despair

"You here!" he softly chided, "you here, what imprudence, what folly!"

Lady Stuart, wan and grief-stricken, advanced towards him.

"Yes, I am here at the Tuileries. Do you not understand, sire, that I must have a powerful motive to risk this imprudence—this folly?"

The young woman's voice trembled, and was almost inaudible. The Emperor looked at his mistress, and his dawning smile disappeared. The dramatic attitude of the Countess Ellen alarmed him.

"*Mon Dieu*, what is the matter—? What misfortune has happened to you?"

"An awful misfortune, sire, my child has been stolen."

The sovereign trembled.

"Your child has been stolen?"

"Yes, it happened fifteen days ago, and I only learned it yesterday, when I went to La Verrière."

The young lady then gave her lover a full account of the abduction.

The Emperor turned pale as he listened to

her. He tugged at his moustache, and feverishly paced his cabinet.

Then he stopped and stammered:

"Your child has been stolen—who could have committed this theft, and for what end? Do you suspect anybody who would be capable of taking revenge in such a way?"

Lady Stuart with an effort let fall one word —"Yes."

Napoleon III. was impatient and nervous.

"Speak, madam—the name of this person."

"Your Majesty insists on the name?"

"I must have it—the guilty person whoever it be, shall not go unpunished."

"The guilty person will not be punished, sire; if your Majesty sees that my son is restored to me I shall be satisfied."

"Undeceive yourself, madam—the guilty person shall be chastised. Again I say, speak."

"The person who has caused my son to be carried off and is hiding him, sire, is the Empress."

At these words the sovereign became intensely pale. The accusation made against his

wife was sudden and unexpected. He was
shocked, and quickly going up to the young
woman, he took her by the arm:

"Silence, madam, silence," he said in a very
low voice, "and never repeat what you have
said to me."

Lady Stuart disengaged herself, and gathering courage from the emotion of the Emperor, she replied:

"Pardon my language, sire, but my child
has been taken from me. I want my child; I
want to see him again dead or alive: and until
I see him, I will not cease to proclaim to you
the name of her whom I consider to be the interested instigator of the misfortune which has
befallen me. You impose silence upon me and
you are right, for you can do nothing in regard
to this revelation, for your justice is powerless
against the rank of the guilty person. You do
not doubt my assertions, you know as well as I
the hand which has struck this blow. I have
been banished from the Tuileries, but she desires more; she desires our separation, and to
attain this end she has plotted to torture my

mother's heart: she thought that my grief would henceforth interpose between you and me, and she was right. From to-day, I am only a weeping mother resolved by any sacrifices to regain possession of her missing child."

The Emperor was sincerely moved.

"The misfortune which has happened to you is abominable, frightful," he said, "and you may rely upon my support, to obtain ample satisfaction. Your child shall be found and returned to you. Calm yourself then, I pray you, and for my sake, who have loved you and still love you do not bring the name of the Empress into this horrible affair. I believe and am certain that you are wrong, besides being prompted by your grief to blame the Empress in this case. From a very natural and perfectly legitimate feeling she banished you from Court: she was desirous perhaps of finding some excuse to bring about a rupture between us. But she is a good woman and a mother, and it is inadmissible to impute designs to her of which she would be incapable, and to charge her with a crime. The Empress is a mother. I repeat, and a mother, madam, does not strike a woman, even though she detests her, through her mother's heart."

Lady Stuart shook her head sadly.

"A woman who hates, sire, is capable of attempting anything against the object of her hate. The Empress is a woman in the expression of her feelings, in the same manner as the rest of her sex."

"Do not say that, madam, do not say that," murmured the Emperor.

And he resumed his pacing up and down in his cabinet.

The Countess Ellen was well aware that the interview she had solicited that morning, could only result in a vague promise of help, an affectionate exhortation and the offer of an uncertain hope.

She thanked Napoleon III. for his sympathy, and took her leave.

As she was leaving the cabinet, she fixed her eyes on the Emperor, and this look was full of pity. She felt that this man, that this ruler, was overwhelmed by the terrible anguish which she had made him suffer, and she pitied him because he was not able in the kindness of his nature, to give her any further consolation than the assurance of a secret support; and was unable, situated as he was, to punish the author of the crime whom she had denounced to him.

She resolved by her own energy to supplement the fatal inaction and the feeble intervention of the Emperor: and as soon as she returned home, she coolly discussed the means which she would employ to solve the cruel enigma which confronted her.

Having come to France with the reputation of an adventuress of high rank, without having desired it, Lady Stuart found that she had missed the path that destiny seemed to have traced out for her. Her life had suddenly been diverted in another direction by an unexpected maternity, and was entirely merged in the feelings awakened by this maternity.

This effacement of self, this forgetfulness of all that which formerly placed her in the front rank of the elegant *habituées* of the Court, this sacrifice of her ambition, fortune and pride, had become more absolute since she had experienced sorrow, since her child had been stolen from her, whose innocent caresses she had rapturously enjoyed.

Then a profound reaction took place in her. With a spontaneous renouncement of her former pleasures, and even her smallest dissipations, she swore to consecrate herself to the recovery of her son, and to vengeance for the grief that had been caused her—a vengeance which she wished to be a signal one, and this already in thought seemed to assuage her grief.

Having heard since the abduction and since her interview with the Emperor, from one of the ladies who frequented the Tuileries and whom she had met, of the words spoken by Mme. de Metternich and the declarations of the Empress, she was convinced that the sovereign had guided the criminal hand which had wounded her: and although between the wife of Napoleon III. and herself, there was a difference as much from a social as from a purely feminine point of view, she vowed to herself to punish her, to return her blow for blow, if her tears were not dried by some fortunate chance.

She did not wish, however, to hasten the reprisals, to declare her enmity, prematurely and as she was more eager to regain possession of of her child than to gratify her feelings of revenge, it was to the recovery of the lost child that she directed all her thoughts.

Having received from the Emperor only a lukewarm promise, and phrases of almost commonplace condolence, she felt that if she wished to succeed in her search, she must act with firmness, whilst carefully avoiding any imprudent action which might arouse the distrust of those who were without doubt watching her.

In an interview with the English ambassador she told him of the abominable conspiracy against her safety, and she asked his support in the task which she had set herself.

The diplomatist seemed to take a judicious view of her situation.

"It would appear certain," said he to her, "when I recall your reception at the Tuileries, and the rivalry which was the result of it, and when I remember certain remarks that were made regarding you in the presence of the Empress, that she, in order to put an end to the *liaison* which caused her uneasiness, has been the instigator of the drama at La Verrière. You must then be extremely circumspect not only in the manifestation of your sorrow, but even more so in the steps you take to ascertain the truth, and to recover your son. I am sure that the child is threatened with no danger in the criminal sense of the word. He has been stolen not to kill him as you say Mme. de Metternich advised, but simply and less dramatically to put him out of the reach of the possible tenderness of the Emperor. He is safe, somewhere among good people who are caring for him without troubling themselves about his history. But to obtain the result that you desire, keep in the background; don't let the newspapers get hold of the story. Public curiosity has nothing to do with this, and if you lose your calmness all hope of success would be gone. The Emperor who can secretly aid you, would be obliged to drop you and take no notice of your grief: reasons of State would intervene between him and you, and you must recognize the fact that he could not compromise himself to satisfy you."

The logic of the Ambassador reduced Lady Stuart to despair.

"I want my child . . . I want him," she cried, "even if I must die for wanting him . . . I beg of you to point out to me some more efficacious way than words of advice to recover him."

The diplomatist replied without emotion:

"This advice is necessary, and it was imperative to give it. As to the means to be employed —listen to me. I will introduce you to a secret agent of the Embassy, who is perfectly familiar with Parisian ways, who is well acquainted with the officials at the Prefecture of Police, and to whom I am indebted for signal services. His name is Frépont. You will let him know all the facts in the case, and will leave him to act."

The young woman felt somewhat consoled.

"And when shall I see the agent?"

"To-morrow. He will call on you; but he will not come as being sent by me. My name must not be mixed up at all with this intrigue. Of course you understand how unpleasant it would be for me at the Tuileries, if I did not appear to be absolutely ignorant of it."

CHAPTER XII.

LADY STUART, when she left the English Embassy, after having thanked her countryman, felt a moral assurance which gave her confidence in the future, and she feverishly looked forward to the next day.

In the afternoon, the agent referred to by the diplomatist was announced. He was a man of short stature, rather stout, with somewhat the appearance of a tradesman in moderate circumstances, or a well-to-do clerk. His round, rosy face, his snub nose and scanty moustache in no way gave any clue to the nature of his occupation. A close observer, however, would have quickly remarked that his gimlet like, narrow, shifty, greenish, ferret's eyes were not those of a candid individual.

Having listened to the young lady without interrupting her, he still remained silent for some minutes, after she had done speaking. lost in reflection, and turning his hat in his fat, plump hands, which were short and very white and adorned with valuable rings.

At length, he raised his head and looking at the Countess Ellen, he slowly, and as if weighing each word before pronouncing it, expressed himself thus:—

"There are some essential clues lacking in this story, madam, and it will not be easy for us to see our way clearly. The guardians of the child know but one thing: a lady one day came from you, to take away from them the child that you had entrusted to them. They did not ask this lady any questions—did they even get a good look at her?—and gave her the child. There are not sufficient details to start an enquiry. However, do not let us despair. I will go to these good people and will make them talk. Perhaps they will tell me more than they did you. As for the lady in question,— ah, I would give something to have a lock of her hair—it wouldn't be much but it would be better than nothing. Well, we will have that lock and we will make use of it. Considering the high rank of her whom you accuse, the woman who was actively employed in this affair must be of some social standing, one who has some friends at the Prefecture of Police.

Follow my reasoning carefully, madam. The woman who has caused you all this trouble, in order to attain her end, has not had recourse to one of her intimate friends, who would have been frightened at the responsibility that such a mission would impose upon her, but to a woman who is accustomed to fear nothing, to what we call a professional. And this woman can only be one who has relations with the police— above all the political police. She will have acted without even knowing for whom she was acting, and under the orders simply of a chief, or a very high official, certainly. This official will have received instructions from we know whom, and will have had them carried out. You understand we should lose our time in trying to discover this gentleman. I must direct all my efforts then, to finding his accomplice. I have the list as well as the description of the women employed by the police of Paris. By proceeding first with a social classification, and then by a process of elimination, I am pretty sure to put my finger and get my eye on the woman for whom we are looking. If I unearth her, then I shall have to make her talk, and that without doubt will not be a very easy thing. But I have patience and with patience one can succeed in anything. For to-day, it is useless to bother our heads any more. Well, good day, madam. To-morrow I shall be at La Verrière, and I will give you an account of my proceedings."

Lady Stuart listened to the agent attentively.

"Go and act quickly, sir; if you return my dear little boy, I will make you rich. I swear it."

"Thank you for your promise, madam," replied the police officer, as he was leaving the room: "although I have some fortune, I am not unwilling to have more. But on my word, this is such a beautiful case, that I would undertake it for the honor alone."

The next day, as he had declared, agent Frépont alighted at the station of La Verrière, and made his way to the house of the former guardians of little Jack.

The man and woman were at home when he presented himself at the door. From Lady Stuart's statement he was convinced of their innocence in the abduction of the child; he wisely decided not to arouse their distrust.

When he entered the house, he said, "It is you with whom the little boy Jack boarded?"

The woman advanced uneasily.

"Yes sir; why this question?"

Without replying to her interrogation, the agent continued:

"I have a message for you. Do you remember a lady who came to your house to take away the child and said that she was sent by the mother?"

"Holy Virgin, do we remember!"

"Well, I have some good news for you. Jack has been found and this time it is really his mother who sends some one to tell you that she grieves no more, and that you need not do so any more."

"Holy Virgin!—ah, Holy Virgin!—" exclaimed the woman, her face radiant, "you are welcome sir. We have done nothing but weep since this happened, and you make us truly happy. So the dear little fellow is found."

"Yes, he is now with his mother, and I assure you that they won't steal him again. The cherub will be taken care of."

The man then spoke.

"The child is found, it is well. But for all that is it known why he was stolen?"

The detective made a gesture of indifference.

"Certainly it is known and it is a very simple thing and there is nothing dramatic about it at all. The lady who came here is a relative of Jack's mother. She has been married and went mad after the death of her husband and an only child. She has a fixed idea that her child is alive. She imagined that the son of her relative was her own, and she made up a plot to carry it off. As this is the second or third time that this fit has seized her and that she has abducted children ; she has been placed under restraint. It is very sad."

The man who had been listening with his mouth open, groaned:

" Poor lady."

" Poor lady, as much as you like," said the detective, "but dangerous all the same."

" Holy Virgin!" said the ex-nurse, "here is an affair. We were worrying our brains, sir, to find out the reason for this abduction and I told the lady that she must be mistaken when she declared that the child had been stolen out of motives of revenge."

And turning to her husband she added triumphantly :

" I was right you see."

The agent interrupted her.

" How is it that you did not perceive that this person was crazy ? "

The nurse a little piqued, replied :

"But my dear sir this woman did not look at all mad. When she first came in, we thought she was our lady. She was young like her and dressed very much like her, it was only when she spoke, for she wore a very thick veil, that we discovered our mistake. She was very polite and there was nothing out-of-the-way in what she said."

"She left you some money?"

"Yes, a large sum, which we dared not touch since we knew that she had stolen the child. My husband wanted to take it to the commissary of police at Rambouillet. But I dissuaded him from this idea: they could have given us trouble. We will return it to you since you are sent by the lady."

Frépont declined to receive it.

"No. Jack's mother wishes you to keep this money, as some compensation for the trouble that you have had."

"Our good lady—you will thank her, sir."

"I will not fail."

There was a silence and then the woman spoke again:

"The relative of our lady as she left, dropped a handkerchief trimmed with lace in the garden, sir. When Jack's mother came here the last time we were in such trouble that we did not think of showing it to her. She would perhaps have recognized it as belonging to her relative, and that would have immediately explained everything,—but one does not think of everything. Since you know to whom to return it, would you kindly take it away? It is a costly trifle."

The agent felt a thrill, which he immediately repressed.

"Give me the handkerchief, my good woman," he said carelessly. "It shall be returned to the owner."

And extending his hand he received a fine cambric handkerchief, which he placed in one of his pockets, without looking at it.

After some more conversation with the guardians, he rose and bid them adieu.

When he was in the train on his way back to Paris, he attentively and with unfeigned delight examined the handkerchief which had been entrusted to him.

It was a costly square of cambric, trimmed as the good woman had said with magnificent lace, with two M's. interlaced, embroidered in the corner.

"Come," murmured Frépont, "our thief is a fine lady, accustomed to elegance. That is an established fact, and my task will be easier than I thought."

Then he added between his teeth, smiling and stroking the handkerchief:

"Little handkerchief, if I am not very much mistaken, you will be the means of drawing a good many things from certain pretty mouths, that they would rather not disclose."

CHAPTER XIII.

The Emperor was very uneasy after the visit of Lady Stuart, and the conversation which he had had with her.

The abduction of a child in which he was deeply interested complicated the situation in which his *liaison* with the young woman had placed him—and as he did not doubt—he confessed it to the Countess Ellen later—that the Empress was indeed the instigator of the plot, and the author of the tragedy; he was embarrassed as to the stand he should take in case the intimate friends of the Empress should discuss the matter in his presence.

This stand was plainly indicated and the Emperor resigned himself to submit to it: he could not appear to be mixed up in such a matter, and the most absolute reserve was necessary in spite of the grief he felt.

He had, however, a second time sent M. Hyrvoix to his grief-stricken mistress, with instructions to consult with her as to the measures to be taken by the police, in order to arrive at a satisfactory result in the search for the child. But when he learnt from his devoted servant that the young woman had not awaited his assistance before acting, he concluded to interfere no further.

Several days then passed without the Emperor and Lady Stuart having the least communication with each other.

Napoleon III. loved his mistress, and this sudden interruption of their relations sincerely grieved him. The time even came when it was difficult for him to endure it, and one evening, braving every obstacle, in his imprudent and affectionate desire to see the young lady again, as also with the intention of acquainting her with certain details relating to the drama at La Verrière, which had come to his knowledge in the palace, he went to her house.

Lady Stuart who was very impatient at the unavoidable delays in the inquiry instituted by Frépont, was very sad and discouraged when the Emperor called upon her, and he only half succeeded in restoring a part of her hope.

"You have anticipated me," he said to her, "in employing a detective to conduct the search for your son. I should have been glad indeed to place the services of one of the agents in my personal service at your disposal to assist you. But this agent could not have done better than yours, and I deplore my inability to be more directly of service to you."

When the Countess Ellen thanked him, he replied:

"I am afraid that this story, some fine morning, will make a scandal in the newspapers. It has already caused me some uneasiness: the consequences of its exposure would be terrible for the Tuileries."

Lady Stuart raised her eyes to the Emperor.

"You have had troubles on my account, sire?"

"Yes. Troubled by the accusations which you recently brought with so much force against the Empress, I wished to know if they had any foundation, and I tried to interrogate her whom you accused."

"Well."

"Well, madam, not only did the Empress from her replies seem to me to know nothing of the real causes of your affliction, but it brought on an explanation between her and me. She bitterly reproached me for my weakness towards you, and threatened to leave the Tuileries—such a threat has already had its effect—if I ever ventured even to mention your name."

"The Empress, sire, in employing against you and me the language of a jealous or a clever woman, has in no way refuted my accusations, and I still persist in thinking that she alone has been the cause of what has happened."

The Emperor continued:

"Truly, the mind becomes bewildered in this affair: if I examine the reasons which you have adduced, and supported by your assertions, it seems to me as you say, that the Empress has plotted the abduction of your son. But if I oppose to these reasons, her attitude, her indignation and anger, her astonishment even, which she manifested when I asked her if she had any clue to the mystery surrounding this drama, I must believe in her perfect innocence. 'I know nothing about the person of whom you speak to me, and I do not wish to know anything about her. This person complains that her son has been stolen. If she had taken good care of him, which was her duty as a mother, he would not have been separated from her.' Such were the words of the Empress. A woman who expresses herself thus, with this harshness of manner towards a weeping mother is not a guilty woman. Besides I declare that nothing in her manner during our conversation, was of a nature to confirm your suspicions. No emotion, no embarrassment betrayed her secret thoughts. If such a secret existed in the breast of the Empress, it would have revealed itself by some look or movement which could not have escaped me. One can hardly attribute to her a knavery which is so little in accord with her general character."

Lady Stuart who had listened to the Emperor coldly and with perfect calmness, replied :—

" You defend the Empress, sire, and in that you do well : you do what every gallant man would do in your place, when he speaks of his wife in the presence of her who is only his mistress. But I regret that I do not share your optimistic belief. The future certainly will show that you are deceived."

The Emperor did not reply, and in a profound melancholy left Lady Stuart.

CHAPTER XIV.

The year 1869—the last but one of the reign of the Emperor Napoleon III.—was troubled, as is well-known, by political movements hostile to the imperial dynasty and all were filled with apprehension at the uncertainty of the future.

The Emperor then suffered more than anyone else in this state of affairs from uneasiness of mind, but, as though by a sort of fatality, his wish to counteract the perils which he foresaw, was almost annihilated by a succession of domestic dramatic events which had for a stage the Tuileries, and for the actors some of his intimate friends.

The tragic event which sprang from the rivalry between the Empress and Lady Stuart, was, indeed, not the only one of the kind, which was revealed at this time, and if it presents a more romantic aspect than the analogous events which were so numerous, at the same time still it would be curious to relate some of them.

I will only relate one of them because in its recital it gives a vivid idea of that feverish life which characterized the members of the Court, and the life at the Tuileries.

I am about to tell of the scandal which compelled one of the most intimate companions of the Empress—she who was known as the beautiful Comtesse de B — to leave the Court, and the sanguinary consequences which followed it.

Mme. de B. who was one of the most charming ladies of the palace of the Empress Eugénie, was not the less eager in taking her part in the pleasures of all kinds which were offered to the *habitués* of the Château, and if she was justly renowned for her elegance and her beauty, she was equally so for her daring *amours*. She was as much talked about at the palace for her easy virtue as for her physical perfection.

The wife of General B., she cared but little for the jealousy of her husband, and she surrendered herself without restraint to all love affairs which fell in her way.

For a long time the General said nothing, but

there came a time when his patience was exhausted and gave place to an anxious care for his dignity.

As long as his wife had appeared to him to be only imprudent, he paid no attention to the reports which he heard about her, and he disdained to interfere and exert his authority. But the conduct of Mme. de B. soon became so shameless, and the scandals about her so precise, and so circumstantial, that he could no longer remain inactive or silent.

He could not doubt that like many husbands he was being deceived, and he determined to know who was the lover of his wife.

One evening, when they returned from the Tuileries, instead of bowing to the countess at the threshold of her door, he passed through the door and resolutely seated himself near her.

. Mme. de B., who had not for several months lived with her husband, was much astonished at this unforeseen attack from so insignificant a foe, and one who even seemed to be complaisant, and it was not without irritation that she asked the General the reason for the surprise.

M. de B.'s answer was very explicit.

"Madam," said he, "you have a lover and I am here to ask you to tell me his name."

The countess, who had not expected a jealous scene, but attributed the visit of her husband to a caprice, a return of his passion for her, was a little taken aback. Her irritation increased and made her awkward, for in place of laughing at the whim of the General, or being indignant at it, as is customary under such circumstances, as so many wives know, she affected a sarcastic air, and amused herself by further torturing the poor man by feigned confessions.

"Truly," said she, "you have learned that I have a lover, and you wish me to give you his name?"

The General made an affirmative gesture.

"And wherefore this desire," continued the countess. "It can only arise from unkind motives. Well, supposing I tell you this name, what would you do? You are a dissembler, and are not skilled in concealing your thoughts —I believe you would kill the man I should name."

M. de B. was a single-hearted man of a frank, straightforward nature. He did not understand his wife's raillery and he replied imprudently :

" Perhaps."

The countess sneered.

" Then I won't give you the name."

The General's calmness was exhausted, and the countess, who had only known him as a confiding and attentive husband, could no longer have any doubt of the violence of which he was capable.

She had scarcely uttered her refusal, when the General seized her violently, bruising her flesh, as, half-suffocated with rage, he gasped threateningly :

" You will tell me this name—I insist on it—. And when I know it, I will kill, yes, I will kill the miserable man who bears it—You have guessed correctly—I will kill him like a dog."

Mme. de B., agitated and terrified, tried to

escape from the grasp of her husband, but he gripped her with so terrible a hold that it was impossible for her to free herself, while he still kept repeating the same words, as though under the influence of a hallucination:

" The name—the name—the name?"

At last despairing of obtaining any information from his wife, who remained mute, and submitted to his violence, with one push he cast her far from him, and began to reflect.

" This man must have written to you," he growled. "Not only do I insist on his name, but you must hand me his letters."

And as Mme. de B. remained motionless:

" Come," he said, " obey, or I swear to you I will have them even if I am obliged to smash everything here to find them."

This scene threatened to have no outcome, for the last sentence pronounced by the General precipitated the *dénouement*.

The countess, whether from a feeling of fear, weariness or refined perfidy—who can analyze the thoughts of a woman at certain times?— suddenly rose and pointing out with her finger to her husband, a piece of furniture, murmured:

" Please do not break anything whatever. I have letters, it is true: they are in the chiffonnier. Open it and search—here is the key."

The General had no trouble in possessing himself of the secret correspondence of his wife. She had not lied. She possessed love letters, and these letters were all in the piece of furniture which she had pointed out.

Only as they were in packages, and as there were four of them M. de B. had the curiosity to compare the hand writings, and finding that the writing in all of them was different, he pushed his investigations further, when he experienced a surprise which he could not possibly have foreseen. In place of one lover, his wife had four; a celebrated Ambassador, M. le Chevalier Nigra; a young colonel of cavalry. M. de G. as famous for his gallantries as for his pranks which they tolerated at the Tuileries; M. le Comte de L., a sportsman; and M. le Marquis de C., a Chamberlain: these last possessors of enormous fortunes.

Amazed, the General turned over the letters in his hands, and was silent. The countess whose frivolity was incorrigible profited by this minute of quietness to recover her liberty, and ready this time for flight if her husband again became violent. She defied him.

"Well, you are satisfied, and I hope you are going to leave me in peace now. You wanted me to give you the name of one lover: I offer you four. You remember the proverb; an abundance of wealth——."

With a hasty movement the General threw the letters back into the drawer of the chiffonnier, and without replying to the raillery of his wife, left the room.

But this incident had an epilogue. The General fought with the lovers of his wife, who were astonished to learn of their collaboration in the loves of Mme. de B. He fought with the Chevalier Nigra, with Colonel de G., with the Marquis de C., and lastly with the Comte de L., who killed him with a sword thrust through the heart.

There was a scandal at the Tuileries. The

affair was known to the newspapers, but they were compelled to abstain from commenting on it under pain of suppression, and the Emperor, by the advice of his ministers, determined to concoct a fable to explain the death of General de B., who died according to order from heart complaint.

This story, in combination with so many other identical ones, shows, I repeat, with what recklessness the women who surrounded the Empress abandoned themselves to the life of folly and sensuality which was the very existence of the Court: it equally shows with what contempt for the future, though it was then sufficiently gloomy, they continued to revel like unconscious, swooning sultanas in the arms of their lovers, protected by the Empress whom these intrigues even though dramatic, amused.

Lady Stuart knew of the incident of Mme. de B.; and while she regretted it when she thought of the sorrow it would cause the Emperor, she rejoiced, because of the hate which she bore to the entire feminine circle of the Empress. This incident could not but cast discredit on this circle, and it revenged her somewhat for the disdain and envy of which she had been the victim at the Tuileries—and for the hypocritical scruples which her own story had excited.

As all her thoughts were for her missing son, she did not linger long over the satisfaction which this scandal gave her, and soon forgot it, to devote herself wholly to the task which she had undertaken.

This task as Detective Frépont had said was a thankless, and difficult one, and almost impossible to accomplish in accordance with the terms of the vow made by the interested party.

CHAPTER XV.

Since the visit of the detective to La Verrière, and the interview that the young lady had had with the Emperor, many days fruitless in results had passed, waiting for a clue, for an event which permitted of hope for a successful issue.

Detective Frépont was clever, however, and was not discouraged. He held one of the threads to the plot which had been hatched against Lady Stuart, and he declared with energy that in spite of the frailty of the thread, he would find the key to the drama by its aid, and recover the child.

He frequently saw Lady Stuart to give her an account of his progress, and to combat the sadness and dejection which oppressed her. The Countess Ellen listened to him, but her sadness increased in proportion as time passed, without a solution, and it seemed as if it was only through politeness that she henceforth replied to his assurances of success.

"I feel I am going to die," she said to him. "Go, my good Frépont: and make haste and find my poor little one, if you wish me to be able to embrace him again. Sorrow will kill me."

Frépont who was a good fellow, and who was sincerely devoted to Lady Stuart, inwardly grieved at her increasing despair. He left her declaring, that he "would assuredly bring her some news the next time," and, when he was obliged to report to her again the failure of his efforts, he hesitated to cross the threshold of her hotel.

Lady Stuart had hated the Empress ever since she suspected her of being the instigator of the abduction of her son. But Lady Stuart was a mother, and a mother, in the love which she bears her child, can not only forget her anger, but she can humiliate herself before him or her who has made her suffer, if she believes that this humiliation may be favorable to the mitigation or removal of her grief.

It was in this state of mind that the young lady, one day, recognizing the slowness of the enquiry instituted by the detective, and being convinced of its fruitlessness, determined to go and find the Empress and beseech her on her knees to pardon her for a rivalry which she regretted ; to beseech her to tell her as a reward for so much abnegation and wounded pride, what she had done with her child. The Empress was a mother. She would certainly forget the insult which Lady Stuart had inflicted on her, and would restore her that son for whom she distractedly extended her arms—that son whom in a spirit of reprisal, she had snatched from her. She would take her child, separate herself from the Emperor, would leave Paris, France,—Europe even,—she would live only for her dear little one, and would bless her who after having made her unhappy, who after having punished her for an audacity which she ought never to have manifested, would grant her peace, life, joy.

This resolution haunted her the whole of one afternoon. But towards evening, when the shades of night were falling around her, her angry sorrow brought about a reaction of ideas in her, and she was indignant at the thought of crawling vanquished to the feet of her, who had not hesitated to strike her such a cruel blow. Then she recovered all her fierce energy, told herself that detective Frépont was right, that her child would be found, and that she should oppose to the hatred, which pursued her, a hatred as intense and as much to be feared, and not the submission of a sentimental woman, of a daughter chastised and repentant.

And then in the gradual exaltation of her thoughts, she gave a cry, a terrible cry. She turned toward the palace which sheltered her enemy and took an oath that if she were destined to cherish her maternal sorrow for ever, to revenge herself, even if in the execution of her vengeance she should be compelled to cause a terrible scandal, by making a direct attack on the person of the Empress: though she should be obliged to kill her who had stolen her happiness from her, who had plunged an inextricable thorn in her heart, which each day pierced deeper into the flesh and deluged her with blood. In her nervous excitement she did not ask herself what they would do with her after the attempt—after the drama. They might cause her to disappear, shut her up in a madhouse, even kill her. Her fate mattered little. She wished for revenge, and her whole soul was bent on the end which she contemplated.

As nothing occurred to change the course of her feelings, and as the detective Frépont, who alone could have procured her some relief, could offer her nothing but vague assurances of success, she gave him no hint of the project which she meditated. She busied herself in making arrangements for this project, to prepare for this senseless design, which hurried her in spite of herself towards irreparable violence.

About this time, Parisian correspondence addressed to foreign journals and some French papers, spoke with uneasiness, and much mystery of a strange event which recurred each time that the Empress left the Tuileries for a promenade.

These journals stated that there was great uneasiness at the Château among the suite of the sovereigns, as well as at the Prefecture of Police, with regard to a woman dressed in black, her face concealed by a somewhat thick veil to avoid recognition, who unwearyingly watched the movements of the Empress, boldly advancing until she touched the carriage when she perceived her.

This woman looked like a living statue of despair and by her muteness and ghostly immobility seemed so threatening that she alarmed those who had charge of the sovereign.

As for the Empress the first appearances of the woman in black did not disturb her. She paid no more attention to this sorrowful apparition, than to those who usually crowded around her horses to look at her. But soon the attitude of the woman interested her more. Her eyes having met those of the woman, she thought she saw a glance of hatred flash from behind her impenetrable veil and she was afraid. The Empress it is known, was not given to fear—to an acknowledged fear, proceeding from a natural and palpable fact. But she was superstitious and the sudden advent, the ominous appearance of a mysterious being, a stranger to her life, troubled her. At first, she refused to see in this almost daily apparition, anything but an incident due to an unlucky accident: then the woman in black existed in her imagination as a funereal vision, haunted her hours of solitude, and she began to dread meeting her, as one dreads an evil omen, and even to avoid going out, for fear of brushing against her mourning garments.

The Emperor who was informed of this fact,

and to whom the worry of the Empress was related, ordered an investigation, and commanded that he should be informed of the name and address of the woman.

The answer which his police officers made him, terrified him. The woman in black who was spreading such consternation in his suite and in the mind of his wife, was Lady Stuart.

He did not at all doubt that the attitude of this woman who was until recently, his mistress, concealed some tragic design, some attempt against the Empress, and he resolved to avert the trouble of which he had a presentiment.

Once more he despatched M. Hyrvoix to Lady Stuart, to beg her by the remembrance of the affection which he had had for her, of the sympathy which he had lavished on her to cease making these dramatic appearances before the sovereign.

The Emperor could have made use of his authority, in spite of the bonds which had united him to the young woman, to compel her to put a stop to these doings. He contented himself with begging her to obey him, and this apparent deference which he showed her then touched her sincerely.

Without renouncing her vengeance, she took into consideration the worry which she was unjustly causing the Emperor in acting thus and she desired M. Hyrvoix to tell him that his wishes would be respected.

She appeared indeed no more before the Empress who, freed from this annoying siege, quickly forgot her uneasiness, as her capricious nature forgot so many other things, frivolous or grave.

Although she had yielded to the Emperor's wish in relieving the sovereign from the intolerable punishment which she was pleased to inflict upon her, Lady Stuart taxed her ingenuity to devise a means of implacably avenging herself. In her stress of mind, she planned the most extravagant and impracticable designs. It was thus she conceived the project of forming a plot for the abduction of the Empress, to seize her person, and having her in her power to force her to reveal the whereabouts of her child.

She knew the habits of the Empress. She knew that her enemy occasionally went out in the morning simply accompanied by one of her ladies, perhaps to visit the shops in the Rue de la Paix, followed at a distance by the famous chestnut-colored coupé, and it seemed to her that under these conditions it would not be difficult to accomplish a forcible abduction. She would spend money freely to secure assistance and she would find some adventurer ready to sell her his support. This plan was foolish: but hate is the mother of follies.

While she was under the influence of this feverish preoccupation, Lady Stuart resolved one day to take vengeance herself without the aid of a mercenary arm.

One morning passing the Rue de Rivoli and walking along the railing of Tuileries, followed by her carriage, the horse going at a walk, parallel with her, she suddenly came face to face with the Empress, who when she saw her, stopped and turned pale.

The two women for a second, measured one another with their eyes: then an uncontrollable rage seized Lady Stuart, and she prepared to demand an explanation from which would result the confession she had waited for so long.

If the Empress did not quite understand the drama which was about to be played, she at least understood the falseness of her position. Justly frightened too at the attitude of the Countess Ellen, she tried to shun the meeting, and getting behind the lady who was with her, she looked around for her coupé.

At that moment, the only carriage near her was that of Lady Stuart. Mistaking it for her own, she ran to the door and opened it.

Then the Englishwoman uttered a cry of triumph. At a bound, she reached the Empress and was already about to push her into the carriage, when her attendant who was observing this scene without entirely understanding the importance of it, approached the Empress and said:

"The Empress is mistaken—that is not her coupé."

The young woman quickly recoiled and avoiding the clasp of Lady Stuart, she walked away swiftly.

This incident passed so rapidly that those who witnessed it did not remark its dramatic character. It remained the secret of the interested parties and the premature and unforseen miscarriage of the plan which she meditated, caused a reaction in the mind of the Countess Ellen. She saw that henceforth she must avoid any public scandal which had for its end the placing of her whom she hated at her mercy; she understood that prudence, the most absolute prudence, would answer her purpose better in the search for her son, than threats which were not easy to put into effect or even acts of violence which could be executed. She again placed all her hope in detective Frépont and awaited from him, with resignation, the word which would restore her her happiness or would kill her.

CHAPTER XVI.

If detective Frépont seemed to be slow in his investigation, in reality, he was losing no time.

As he had told Lady Stuart after his visit to the former guardians of Jack, the woman who abducted the child must have been a woman of fashion although connected with the police: and having decided upon the plan of his investigation, he entered upon the campaign for her discovery, furnished only with the feeble clue which he possessed—the precious handkerchief which had been entrusted to him.

Under various plausible pretexts, he visited the majority of the women whom he knew to be secretly attached to the police, and tried to solve the mystery which confronted him. But nothing in the words or the actions of these women, nothing in their personal belongings had given him the information which he desired.

The handkerchief was ornamented with two interlaced, embroidered M's. Frépont first of all visited the women whose surnames and Christian names corresponded with these initials. Having met with no success in this direction, he had not hesitated to visit those whose names did not correspond with the telltale initials. A woman, he argued with reason, may make use of some article—such as a fine handkerchief—which not having been intended for her, bears the initials of some other person.

In thus going to these different women, he was very careful to make no mention of the La Verrière drama: but he hoped that one of them, in the course of conversation might place him on the hidden track for which he was looking; that one of them might, perhaps, display a handkerchief similar to that which he carefully preserved, and would thus betray her guilt.

His investigations were fruitless. Frépont began to ask himself if he would not be wise in abandoning a trail which became less and less clear, and if he had not cherished a vain hope in taking for the basis of his operations the elegant rag dropped in the garden at La Verrière. In his doubt and hesitation he was preparing to give a new direction to his investigation, when an incident which he could not foresee—one of those incidents which are often of more service to men than all the ability and science in life—confirmed his first convictions and gave a fresh impetus to his suspicions.

Having been summoned to give some information to the residence of one of the most prominent public men of the day, the most feared at the Tuileries for his implacable opposition to the imperial power—M. E. de G., and having been shown into his room, Frépont of a sudden espied in a drawer in which M. de G. was rummaging, a fine piece of linen lying in a corner among his papers. It seemed to him that this rag had some analogy with that in his possession, and he determined not to be content with a simple probability, and not to leave without having discovered his mistake, or proved the subtlety of his instinct as a detective.

By a movement of M. de G., in turning over the things contained in the drawer, the handkerchief fell on the floor.

Frépont—whom circumstances were decidedly favoring—picked it up and feigning indifference, was about to replace it, when he stopped. Affecting a tone of Parisian *blague* and holding the handkerchief between two fingers, by one of the corners, so as to completely unfold it, he said jokingly:

"It appears there are all sorts of things in your drawer, M. de G., even love tokens——"

"What are you saying?" replied the journalist.

"Nothing but what is flattering to you I suppose. What do you call that trifle there if not a love token? You cannot make me believe that it was made for your use——"

While he was speaking thus, the detective had an opportunity to examine the handkerchief, and he was filled with an intense joy. It was an exact reproduction of the one in his possession. He must learn the name of the woman who had left it at M. de G's. house, and he employed all his art to induce his interlocutor to mention her name.

M. de G. laughed lightly at the familiarity of the detective.

"No, assuredly, M. Frépont," said he, "I will not tell you that I blow my nose with such precious things. Would to God that I had never seen the nose that has been rubbed with that."

"A knavish little nose that has been faithless, eh?" the detective remarked. "That is a nice affair. Does one ever regret having known a pretty woman?"

"One does regret to have known a hussy."

"Men are all alike," the detective exclaimed; "as soon as a woman deceives them—hard words."

M. de G. became interested in this conversation which awoke memories of the past. He turned towards Frépont and fixing his eyes on him, said:

"I repeat to you that the woman to whom this handkerchief belonged, is a hussy. Besides you know her better than I do."

" I know her?"

"Certainly. She is one of the most adroit assistants at the Ministry of the Interior, in the department of the Political Police, and my little secrets have come out through her."

" What are you telling me?"

" The truth."

" You puzzle me."

" The woman in question is named Martha Masson."

Frépont at this moment, made an involuntary movement, the cause of which M. de G. misunderstood.

" You see you know her," he continued. " The first time I saw her it was at the office of the paper where she came to propose to me some society articles—or rather articles about the *demi-monde*. I did not accept her articles, but asked her for something else, which she willingly granted me. I ought to have been suspicious of this too rapid submission. She is charming. I was in love with her and she came to my house. Then one night when she thought I was asleep, I surprised her standing in her night-dress in the middle of the room with some papers in her hand. I jumped out of bed and went to her and in the explanation which took place between us it appeared that taking advantage of my confidence and when I was asleep, she had rummaged in my cabinet and had robbed me of very important letters and documents. Was that her *début* in violating my confidence? I don't know yet. I turned her out without insisting upon her giving me an account of her past which I think she would scarcely have confessed. She left this handkerchief with me. I shall not be the one to return it to her."

The detective was radiant. At last he held the key to the mystery, which he had so long despaired of discovering; but he preserved his joking air of good-nature, and while pleading extenuating circumstances for the mistress of M. de G., he replied:

" Perhaps you are wrong to be alarmed. This poor girl whom I know indeed (on the the contrary, her name was not on his list) did she really play this melodramatic part in your house that you attribute to her?"

The journalist burst out laughing.

"See here, my dear Frépont," cried he, "if you capture a gentleman in the act of picking your pocket, and taking your purse, would you not see in him a thief?"

The detective did not wish to enter into a discussion with M. de G., regarding the virtue of Mlle. Martha Masson.

He answered evasively, and concluded:

"It is a strange story. It is probably the most innocent in the life of that woman. You ought to know some things about all these '*gaillardes*' in the pay of the authorities."

"Yes."

And after a pause, the detective added:

"There are some among them who have committed crimes."

As he said this he handed the handkerchief to M. de G., and it disappeared in the drawer from which it came.

That same day in the evening, detective Frépont presented himself at the house of

Lady Stuart, and narrated to her the facts which had come to his knowledge.

The young woman was so delighted to hear the news, that the detective feared she might commit some imprudence.

"Yes," said he, "I believe that this time we have our hands on our unknown woman. To-morrow, I will go to her house: we will then have an interview and decide on the course which we must pursue. Henceforth, madam, I shall not be the only one to act, and you will be my assistant. I beg of you to control your feelings of satisfaction, as the least imprudence would render all our efforts abortive. Remember that the woman of whom I speak is one skilled in intrigues, and in every kind of trick, and that one word, an unguarded movement will suffice to let her know who we are and to upset all our plans!"

The woman who had been brought to the notice of Frépont by an unforeseen accident, Mlle. or rather Mme. Martha Masson, enjoyed a certain celebrity among the *demi-monde* during the Second Empire, and was under diverse circumstances one of the ablest auxiliaries of the political police at that time.

Very pretty, a woman of fashion, she held an envied position, in the fast world, and she employed in the choice of her *liaisons*, a method, a circumspection, and an importance which never played her false. As a matter of fact, only men of high position enjoyed her favors. She was from time to time, the mistress of a foreign ambassador, or of certain deputies or public men belonging to the republican party, then of a noble duke, reigning over the faubourg St. Germain, under the name of " Roy," and then of a faithful adherent of the Prince of Orleans, whom it was said she arranged to meet as he left the receptions of the Duchess de Galliéra. This personage although of a ministerial aspect was not insensible to feminine wiles. He saw her, was conquered, and as the pretty woman had hoped became her slave.

Thus Martha Masson was allied at that time with all the parties adverse to the imperial dynasty, as well as with some factions in the foreign colony. Clever as she was she managed to conceal from her lovers the secrets of her life, and, though it is reasonable to suppose that they did not converse of their political business, she nevertheless had opportunities in their relations of picking up a chance word or a scrap of writing which she could utilize.

A man, no matter what his rank or his prudence, is never beyond committing an indiscretion, and when this indiscretion takes the shape of a pretty woman, the time will come without doubt when his confidence will be betrayed.

Martha Masson found her occupation in conjunction with the secret police congenial. Intelligent, of an adventurous mind, she was glad to hunt up mysteries as long as she could reap a profit from them. Indeed, she was well paid for her services, and by her occult influence she was not far from being a real power. Women of the class of Martha Masson, were not rare under the Second Empire. The imperial dynasty which relied so much upon woman from a worldly point of view, employed women, in almost all the phases of its continuance.

It was known that Mme. la Comtesse de R. one of the Empress Eugénie's suite, was an ardent politician and devoted her marvellous intelligence to the pursuit of politics. It was equally well known that Mme la Baronne de B., whose exclusive receptions were celebrated and even feared, subsidized as they were by the secret funds, stood high at the Ministry of the Interior, and the Department of Police.

It would take a volume to give a list of all the women who under the second empire, revolved around the sovereign under the direction of M. Piétri and his predecessors, and to give an account of the comedies or dramas which were the result of their secret participation in public matters. The police woman at that time was recruited from all classes of society, but principally from among the aristocrats and the most conspicuous of the *demi-monde*. From their multiple relations, these women were in a position to pick up information which while it was sometimes useless to the government, giving information in advance of a plot or intrigue, and the state of the public mind, was never to be despised.

It was an open secret in the drawing-rooms of the aristocracy or those of the *demi-monde* that the police-woman—the spy—to use the popular expression—existed; but they were rarely discovered, and it was due to the uneasiness occasioned by the possibility of their presence, that the mistrust existed which characterized the men of the Second Empire. Above all, in the last years of its existence was developed this distrust. It was impossible to go to a ball, or a party, or a fête without being suspected of being a conspirator, and the most gracious speeches as well as the softest looks were suspected. Happy at that time, were those who being nothing or wishing for nothing from the State, took their pleasure with the idea only of enjoying to the fullest the nights or days of pleasure offered to them.

Miss Martha Masson at that time was one of these women; but was she the woman of whom detective Frépont was in search, who, as Lady

Stuart thought, had been the unconscious and passive instrument of the hate of the Empress?

This was the problem to be solved by the detective. As he had told his employer, the day after his conversation with her, he called at the house of Miss Masson, who occupied a very luxurious apartment in the Monceau quarter, in a newly constructed building, conspicuous from its scarcely dried mortar.

The detective rang the bell, of the pretty girl, in the morning. This hour seemed to him to be the most favorable for his expedition. He thought indeed that Miss Masson still in bed or at her toilette, would receive him, and that when alone with her it would be easy for him to pick up some clue to the case of which he had charge.

He was not deceived. Miss Masson engaged with her powders and her perfumes, when he was announced, asked him to wait for her for a moment.

She was dressed and charming when she entered the room, and the detective was almost overcome by her beauty. His profession as well as the motive which took him to her house did not permit of any gallantries, and he left to chance the opportunity for furnishing an excuse for his visit, when he experienced a somewhat unpleasant surprise.

Miss Masson before commencing the conversation, said:

" When they told me just now that a gentleman wished to see me I was far from thinking of you."

The astonished detective stammered:

" You know me, madam ? "

" Yes, you are Mr. Frépont, and I don't suppose that it is for the pleasure of seeing me that I am indebted for your visit."

" It would be a pleasure," replied the detective who had recovered his sang-froid, and who saw that he could not conceal his identity, "but you are right : I am charged with a mission for you."

And he added : " You see, madam, that I have the happiness of knowing you." These words placed the interlocutors on an equal footing.

Miss Masson manifested no surprise when she learned that her secret functions were known to Frépont, besides it did not appear singular to her that an agent should know her since she knew him herself.

"What is your mission to me," she asked.

The detective pretended to recoil: then he drew near to the pretty girl, and leaning over her, affected a confidential tone:

"A pretty delicate mission," he murmured. And purposely employing the slang of his trade, he continued:

"You 'work,' as I do, more for the government than for private individuals. In the case in which I am engaged it is a private individual who requires your services, if you decide to assist me. She is rich and will pay well."

Miss Masson made a face.

"I don't much like having to do with private individuals: one is obliged in dealing with them to come out of one's shell, and the compensation does not always make up for the imprudence which one commits."

The detective stopped her.

"The person employing me does not know that I am at your house now. I am entrusted with the conduct of a certain matter and I am here on my own account. If you refuse to help her, she will never know of my visit. If you consent to aid her, the pleasure you will give her will assure you her gratitude."

"What is the nature of the case?"

It was necessary to invent a story and the detective was equal to the task.

"A foolish business enough, in truth. A lady has a husband whom she does not love and whom she cannot bear. She wants a separation from him. But as he gives her no pretext for bringing suit, she is determined to make one. He must be caught in an intrigue with a woman. Will you play the rôle of the woman? Are you willing to brave a small scandal and the risk of being caught in *flagrante delicto?* If so, it will be easy for you under a feigned name and under some pretext to establish the necessary relations with the husband. You will not be left together long. The wife will surprise you and will make a scene: your false lover will become indignant, and will swear he is innocent. You will be free to imitate him. But you will not be believed, the appearances will be against you and the game will be up. The separation which is impossible to-day will be accomplished to-morrow."

Miss Masson listened attentively to the detective.

"It is not a complicated matter," she said when she spoke. "But why have you selected me for an accomplice in such a simple matter? The first woman you met would have served you as well as I."

Frépont suppressed a nervous movement, for the logic of the *demi-mondaine* perplexed him. But he replied to her with a good-natured air:

"You are mistaken; the first woman I meet would not do: she might be awkward or she might be unwilling to engage in an intrigue. With you there will be a scandal. Your worldly position and your name will cause the matter to be talked about, and the person for whom I am acting will benefit for all these reasons."

Then he added with an air of honest respect:

"Besides I have confidence in you because you are a 'professional' because with you one can be sure that the business will not be a failure and I would never dare to associate with me a collaborator in such a case, who did not belong to our trade."

The young girl smiled.

"All right; I accept. When is it to come off?"

Frépont looked cunning.

"The comedy—when? I don't know yet. I had to get your consent first. I have it and that is the chief thing. I must now see my client and tell her that I am ready to do what she wishes. If she is still of the same mind, I will give her your name and we will fix on the day!"

Miss Masson looked hard at the detective.

"And the price?"

"The price? You are right to remind me of that; I had forgotten. When I come and fetch you, I will give you 10.000 francs, and when the curtain falls, you will receive an equal sum. Is that satisfactory?"

The young woman extended her hand to the detective.

" All right."

" Till we meet again."

" Good-bye."

Frépont left Miss Masson after having engaged her for an imaginary adventure, which could only serve his purpose, by bringing Lady Stuart face to face with the girl and trying to establish the fact that she was really the woman who abducted the child, from La Verrière. Although he was not sure of this, his instinct as a detective told him that she must be the woman of whom he was in search, and he decided to act as if he had received her confession. The handkerchief picked up at La Verrière and the one which M. de G. had shown him were sufficient proofs that he was not deceived! And then what had Lady Stuart or he to fear if they were mistaken? Martha Masson would be angry. But she could be conciliated by excuses and a consolatory gift, and she would congratulate herself at an event which gave her so little trouble and brought her so much unexpected profit.

As he left the house he had decided on his plan of action, but as he bent his steps to the house of Lady Stuart, to tell her what he had done, and the *rencontre* he had arranged for, between her and Miss Masson, without the knowledge of that young woman, who thought to play the part of a woman in love, he reflected that he had perhaps better not see the Countess Ellen, and he wrote to her informing her of what he had done.

"In two days," he concluded, "I will go and fetch Miss Masson and will take her to your house. In order to induce her to accompany me to your house or rather to that of the husband with whom I have furnished you, I have promised to pay her 10,000 francs. Please send me this amount without delay. I will not call at your house until the hour for action arrives. Miss Masson is a slippery customer, and may have me watched: she will discover your identity, and she will guess the trap we are laying for her. I will bring her to you in the evening, and by engaging her in conversation, I will try to divert her attention from the route we are following. Be ready then in two days to receive us."

On the other hand, Frépont addressed a laconic note to Miss Masson: " Be at home every evening after you receive these lines. Everything has been arranged and I will come for you at the proper time."

Lady Stuart, when she read the detective's letter, gave a cry of joy and hate—a cry of joy for her child—a cry of hate for the woman who had stolen him from her—and who she did not doubt would soon be crouching on her knees before her pitiless hate.

CHAPTER XVII.

The two days which elapsed between the sending and the receipt of these letters, were two feverish ones for Lady Stuart and the detective.

The hour set for action at length sounded, and on the evening of the second day of waiting, a carriage stopped before Miss Masson's house. The detective alighted, quickly passed the porter's lodge, and soon found the young woman faithful to the appointment she had made with him. When she saw Frépont, she made a movement of pleasure and smiled.

"Do you know," said she to him, "that I was beginning to get tired of staying at home as if I was in prison? You have come to deliver me, I suppose?"

"The matter is fixed for to-night," replied the detective, "and your captivity ends. Are you ready?"

"Look."

At this invitation, the detective looked hard at her. She was well got up to play the part he had invented—the heroine of a love affair. Very simply but coquettishly dressed, her beauty enhanced by the nervous excitement caused by the part she was to play, rendered her supremely seductive.

"You are adorable," said he, "and just what

you ought to be for our intrigue." Then, smilingly, " ah, ha, don't tell me any nonsense: don't let your lover escape before he 'bites.'"

Miss Masson joked in her turn:

" Don't be afraid. The programme will be faithfully carried out. I will not answer for the consequences of the comedy, however, and if I am really going to be loved as you say—"

The detective interrupted her, cynically, and playing his part to perfection:

" You would allow yourself to be loved, wouldn't you? Well, that is not forbidden—on the contrary—"

" Unhappily it is more probable that my unwilling lover will turn me out when he learns that he has been duped."

" Who knows?"

" It is true—who knows—men are so whimsical—"

As she talked she was putting on her street clothing, and was ready for Frépont. But when she was ready to follow him she took him by the arm.

" *Apropos*, my dear Mr. Frépont, it might be

useful for me to know now the name of the gentleman whom I am going to compromise."

The detective slapped his forehead as if reproaching himself for his forgetfulness.

"Pardon me," he said, "I am distracted—we are going to visit Count de Noré."

The young woman seemed to be taxing her memory.

"Count de Noré—that is not much like a Parisian name. For my part, I don't know it."

"There is nothing surprising in that," said the detective, who did not wish to arouse her suspicions. "The Count and Countess de Noré lived in retirement in the country before settling themselves in Paris, where they have only been a short time."

And he added philosophically: "They would have done very much better not to have come here, for Paris, so far as we can judge, does not seem to have brought them happiness."

Miss Masson accepted this natural explanation but remained motionless in front of her companion.

"Well," said the detective, "are you coming; it is time."

"Didn't you promise to give me 10,000 francs when you came to fetch me?"

Frépont roared with laughter.

"Ah, you didn't forget that promise, my sweet child, and you are right The 10,000 francs are in my pocket. They will be yours the moment we cross the threshold of the Hotel de Noré."

"Why don't you give it to me now?"

The detective winked his eyes and looked surly.

"We are not going to be suspicious of one another: that would advance neither the affairs of our client nor our own. I have it—be sure once for all—for I believe we shall have further dealings together. What assurance have I that if I pay you now, you will not make me a curtsy, and give up the little job awaiting you? In such a case what recourse have I against you. Come, no equivocation between us. I will give it to you. Does that suit you?"

"Be it so," she answered dryly. "Let us be off."

And she added, "You will never die of over-confidence, my dear fellow."

This brief discussion of interests, between the detective and his companion caused a slight coolness. She entered the coupé which was standing at her door, curled up in a corner and was nearly silent during the journey from her house to that of Lady Stuart. This sullenness was useful to Frépont who feared that the young woman would be too inquisitive as to where she was being taken and doubtful of the rôle which she had accepted. He left her to her ill-humor and did not address a word to her until the carriage came to a stop in front of the hotel.

He then drew a pocket-book from the inside pocket of his coat and smiling handed it to the young girl.

"We are prompt in our payments," said he. "Here are the 10,000 francs promised. It is now for you to earn them and as much more."

Miss Masson seized the pocket-book and in

the twinkling of an eye satisfied herself that the money was all right. Satisfied with her examination, she attempted to get out of the carriage, but the detective stopped her.

"Let me ring," he said in a low tone: "you must go straight into the house without stopping on the sidewalk."

A rapid scene then ensued —a bell sounded, —a door was opened and two shadows glided into the hotel.

The comedy planned by the detective was now finished, and Lady Stuart was now to come upon the scene.

Miss Masson astonished at the detective entering the house with her, stopped in the hall, and turned to him enquiringly:

"You are coming with me?"

"For a moment. We will go up to the first floor together and as soon as you are there, you will go to the right where the apartments of the Count are and I will go to the left to the Countess' rooms. I will inform her of your arrival and will go down-stairs again. If M. de Noré appears surprised at your not being announced to him, tell him that you have seen his wife and that she showed you his apartment."

Having ascended the staircase without meeting a single servant, the detective and his companion stopped and consulted.

Frépont pointed out a door to the young girl, and said: "It is there," then pushing her towards the door he pretended to go away. But scarcely had Miss Masson half opened the door pointed out to her, than the agent returned and made his appearance in the room behind her. Then there were some exclamations and some confused murmurs. Then a voice—the voice of a woman clear and sharp rang out:

"You did not expect to find a woman here, did you mademoiselle?"

The young girl looked distressed. Without understanding what was required of her, she guessed that she had fallen into a trap, and she felt that some danger threatened her. She cast a look at the detective begging for an explanation of the mystery which she feared and to reproach him for his treachery: but the officer stood immovable in a corner of the room, and did not appear to be disposed to gratify her curiosity.

"What does this mean?" she said: "Where am I? where have I been taken? are you not the Countess de Noré?"

Lady Stuart was very pale and fixed her cruel eyes on the young girl.

"I am not the Countess de Noré I have no husband—You are here for something else than to play the parody of an adulteress."

Martha Masson was terrified and stammered: "Once again, I ask—what does all this that I see and hear mean? The man who stands there brought me to this house to accomplish a mission that I accepted. He whom I was to meet is not here, she whom I was to serve threatens me—I want to leave at once, and if you do not immediately set me free I will scream—I will call for help."

Lady Stuart replied:

"Your voice will not be heard. Refrain from making any noise. You are in my power and no one can protect you from me now."

Angry and frightened, the young girl demanded:

"Will you tell me madam, the reason for this ambush?"

"You shall be satisfied," said Lady Stuart.

Then addressing the detective, she said:

"Frépont, will you kindly show this young lady something which will certainly interest her?"

The detective then came forward and drew from his pocket the handkerchief found at La Verrière and handed it to the young woman.

"Do you recognize this article?" he asked.

The girl took it from the hands of the detective, examined it and said:

"I recognize that this handkerchief is similar to some in my possession, and which were presented to me by a person to whom I was formerly of service. I cannot affirm that more like them are not in existence, and that this one necessarily belongs to me."

The detective interrupted her firmly.

"I affirm that this handkerchief is your property, just as much as one that you forgot at the house of M. de G., when he surprised you rummaging among his papers and put you out. You lost this one at La Verrière, in the garden of the worthy people to whose house you went for the purpose of stealing a child—a little boy named Jack. Come, you don't dare deny that."

The young woman seemed half crushed by the suddenness of this accusation. She now understood all its importance, and the motive for bringing her to this woman, standing before her, and in her fear at the discovery of her identity, she attempted a denial.

"I don't know what you are talking about," she said. "I don't know M. de G., and and I know nothing of the story of the abduction to which you allude."

The dectective became bullying.

"Don't play the innocent, and above all don't attempt to deceive me. We are colleagues, remember, and you are smart enough to know that you cannot dupe me. You have been the mistress of M. de G. and you are the woman who committed the abduction at La

Verrière. Confess frankly; it's the best thing you can do."

Martha Masson became indignant and assumed an air of pride.

"I have been the mistress of M. de G.—that is possible; but that only concerns myself: it has no reference to the handkerchief which you cast in my teeth, as an irrefutable conviction of a crime of which I know nothing."

"It condemns you."

"What are you going to do?"

"This: you must tell us the place where you have taken the child which was given to you at La Verrière. Until you give us this information, you will remain our prisoner."

Martha Masson flew into a violent passion:

"This is truly unheard of! I repeat to you that I am not the guilty person you think me, and I will add that if I were guilty, I should be justified in demanding by what right you offer me violence."

Lady Stuart then took two paces towards the young woman and stood towering over her.

"The young lady is right," she said: "I have

not introduced myself to her." And in a low, deep voice she apostrophized her:

"Miserable, miserable woman, dost thou not understand that she who is now interrogating thee is the mother of the poor child whom thou hast stolen?"

The young girl recoiled. "You the mother—"

"Yes, I Lady Stuart, the mother—the mother—dost thou hear of the little creature whom thou hast stolen, and whom thou wilt restore: if not, vile prostitute, I will slay thee with my own hand."

Before this revelation and this explosion of hate, Martha Masson could not find words to express either her fear or her boldness. Hoarse sounds rattled in her throat, and she instinctively made a rush for the door by which she had entered.

But she ran against Frépont who seized her by the waist and pushed her back into the room. His coolness at this moment contrasted strongly with the excitement of Lady Stuart and the fear depicted in the face of the young girl.

"Madam," said he, "calm yourself. The terror of this girl shows she will confess, and she will soon understand that it will be to her best interests to give us all the information necessary."

Martha Masson standing motionless in the middle of the room looked alternately at the detective and at Lady Stuart, as if trying to learn her fate from their attitude and also debating inwardly whether she should confess or make a fresh denial.

She seemed to be about to open her mouth to speak: but the shock she had suffered was too great for her nerves to resist, and with a terrible, piercing scream, she burst into tears and sobs.

Lady Stuart was in anguish. "We shall know nothing."

Frépont chuckled: "Yes, yes, madam. on the contrary we shall know all that we wish to know. The pretty creature is suffering from a nervous attack—good—good that. If she were innocent do you think she would be fluttering like that?"

As he pronounced these words, Frépont pointed to Miss Masson who, stretched on the carpet was beating the air with her arms and legs suffering from a bad nervous attack.

In the disorder of her movements some feminine belongings fell from the pocket of her dress, among them a sort of note-book closed with a key.

The detective saw it and picked it up. Then as he turned it over between his fingers, as if seized by a sudden resolution he drew a knife with a large blade from the fob of his trowsers, and without hesitation wrenched off the lock of the note-book and commenced to turn over the leaves eagerly.

When Lady Stuart looked at him anxiously, he smiled at her:

"In our business," he murmured, falling into his professional slang, "we men rarely write anything about our business. But the women who are our colleagues, act differently. They generally have a mania for scribbling, and they often betray themselves by this, just as simple-minded women do, who, when they are in love hoard up their letters at the risk of spoiling their love affairs."

He continued his examination of the notebook, and was silent for a minute.

"Hold," he soon said, "what did I tell you? An account of all that this woman has done for some time is given here."

Lady Stuart did not reply, but left the matter to him and seemed to await an unexpected result.

Suddenly the detective exclaimed: "Madam, madam, come here and read."

Lady Stuart flew to his side and leaning over him, read this line to which he pointed with his finger:

"*To take the child to its destination.*"

Above and below these words were accumulated other notes, but nothing explained them. By their brevity and meagerness, there was no room for the writer to deny her guilt.

Lady Stuart in presence of the clearness of the revelation made to her, and the hope held out to her, felt her strength fail her in the hour of victory, felt as faint as she had been strong in the contest, and running to a seat she crouched on it weeping.

The detective was moved.

"Weep, madam," said he good-naturedly, "it will do you good; but you must cry for joy now. My faith! it is just as good as if we had already found the little one."

Then going to Martha Masson who was still stretched upon the carpet but who had quieted down, he took her hands which he patted, and spoke to her in a milder tone as he showed her the note-book.

"No more use denying it. We know all. Come, rouse yourself a little."

The girl heard what Frépont said, and understood that it was useless for her to persist in her denial, and it was suppliantly that she turned to Lady Stuart and gave her a true account of the crime she had committed.

"A woman whom I do not know and whom I could not even recognize, so heavily was she veiled, but who was sent to me by a high official, with an order from the Prefect of Police came to me one evening and ordered me to take the child from La Verrière, and take him to A. near Nancy. I thought that a mystery surrounded the birth of this child, but that it was not my business to seek to penetrate it by asking for explanations. I thought even that you were in accord with the action of the authorities, and I accepted the task which was offered me, without uneasiness as to its probable consequences. I belong to the police and obey the orders I receive. I was guilty but I was less so than you thought. I have served the interests of your enemies, but the excuse for my conduct is wholly due to my ignorance of the facts which resulted from it."

Detective Frépont was delighted.

"Well, haven't I guessed right about this intrigue?" said he. "Hasn't everything turned out just as I supposed? This woman who is at your knees, madam, has committed an abominable action, but she acted by order as a police employee, without knowing the hand which directed the deed, and it is not upon her that your hate should rest."

The professional instinct again came up in

Frépont and he pleaded his own case in pleading that of Miss Masson. Lady Stuart scarcely heard him, however.

"You have taken my son to A. near Nancy," said she: "and I shall again see him there?"

Martha Masson in affright at her new responsibilities, corrected the Countess Ellen:

"It is at A, yes madam, that you should see him again, if events with which I have nothing to do, have not again changed his destiny."

Lady Stuart turned frightfully pale.

"This girl arouses all my fears," she groaned. "To-morrow I shall leave for Nancy."

Then addressing the detective, she added:

"As for you, Frépont, you will remain here until my return, and will not allow Miss Masson to communicate with any one whomsoever during my absence."

"Then, madam," protested the young woman, "I shall still remain your prisoner in spite of my confession, and this is all the reward I shall receive for my frankness."

"Until I find my son again, you will remain in my power, yes," said Lady Stuart. "As for your frankness and the reward which you ought to have for it, do not let us speak of it if you please."

As the young girl looked at the detective with an air of grief she could not conceal, Frépont extended his arms to heaven, and consoled her with this phrase:

"All is not rose-colored in the profession."

CHAPTER XVIII.

Two days after the dramatic scene which took place between Miss Masson and Lady Stuart, the latter armed with the directions furnished to her, arrived at A., a village in the suburbs of Nancy, and knocked at the door of a neat looking cottage, standing a little apart from the other dwellings and which it was easy to recognize without awakening the curiosity of the peasants by imprudent questions.

A woman twenty five years of age came and opened the door to her. Lady Stuart was very much agitated at this supreme moment of her life, but she suppressed her emotion, and it was in a very calm voice that she addressed the woman who presented herself.

"Madam Bernier?" she asked.

"I am she," responded the woman.

"I wish to speak with you."

The puzzled and distrustful peasant woman, surprised at receiving an unexpected visit from so imposing a person as Lady Stuart did not move, and began to ask questions in her turn.

"You want to speak to me? You have made a mistake, perhaps, madam?"

Lady Stuart whose impatience was increasing, assumed an authoritative air.

"I want to speak with you and I have made no mistake," she declared dryly, "since you tell me you are Madam Bernier."

The woman then politely moved out of her way.

"Come in then, madam, and excuse me for having received you like that," pointing to her housekeeper's dress.

The peasant woman was pretty and the

Countess deemed it wise to pay her a compliment to conciliate her.

"You look very nice as you are, my child," she said smiling, while she looked from right to left in the room to which she had been shown: "a pretty girl like you does not require ornaments."

After a short silence, realizing that she must explain the reason for her visit she continued:

"Here is what brings me to your house. You are married and a nurse. In a few months, I shall become a mother, and must find some one living at a long distance from Paris, where I live, to take care of my child. A lady, a friend of mine who knows you has given me your name. I want to know if I can count on you when the time comes for having a nurse."

The peasant who was conciliated by the prospect of making a profit, replied naively:

"Your friend—can it be that lady who left a child with us, some time ago?"

"Exactly," said Lady Stuart, "it is the same lady."

The woman commenced to laugh.

"Ah well, I must say she does not give us much trouble. We haven't seen her since the day she brought us the child."

The Countess thought she could give a good reason for the absence of her supposed friend.

"This lady," said she, "has very grave reasons which prevent her from visiting her child as she would desire, but she hears of him from sources of which you know nothing."

The peasant made a gesture of indifference.

"That is what people are always telling me. There must be some story about the birth of my foster-child. But as these things don't concern me and as the child's board has been paid in advance, higher paid even than it is worth, I have never bothered myself about the rest. When your friend wants her child back, she will only have to come back here for him. She will find him in good health, I can tell you. It will give me real sorrow to separate from him, for I love him well aside from what he is worth to me; but what of that, he does not belong to me."

Lady Stuart let the woman talk and when she was silent, renewed her question:

"Well, nurse, would you like me to give you my child too?"

"Certainly, madam: we are not rich: and ask nothing more than to be able to gain our living."

At this moment, a man about thirty years of age entered the cottage, dressed in working-clothes, as if just come from the fields. He stopped bashfully when he saw Lady Stuart and muttered an embarrassed good-day.

The peasant woman introduced him:

"It is my husband."

Then speaking to the young man as she pointed out the Countess:

"Madam has come," she added, "to make arrangements for another foster-child after this one that I have."

"Much obliged, madam," said Bernier.

And in reply to his wife:

"Will not this fatigue you too much," he asked affectionately, "to rear two infants like that one after the other?"

The peasant woman laughed heartily.

" If that is all that worries you, don't be uneasy—I am not a Parisian, am I?"

This last sentence was uttered without the least idea of any reflection. She immediately regretted it as a taunt directed against her visitor.

" Oh, pardon me, madam." she said blushing and confused, " I do not mean that for you."

Lady Stuart affected gaiety, and seemed to approve the remark.

" You do not vex me my child, and I think you are right: Parisian women are bad nurses."

All these words. the prelude to the coming scene—made the Countess impatient. She decided to come to the object of her journey.

" We are agreed," she continued : " you will bring up my child and you will be well rewarded for the care you give it. I am now going away and will not return for some months. But I have a commission to execute at your house before I go away. My friend told me to kiss her little boy. Would you bring him here?"

The peasant made no objection to this request which seemed to her quite natural.

"I will go and fetch him, madam," she declared.

She added: "but he is asleep and when he is suddenly awakened like that he is not very good."

As she said this she disappeared in an adjoining room to the one in which Lady Stuart was, and soon came out holding in her arms a pretty little boy in a bad temper at having been disturbed from his sleep, crying and gesticulating with all the power of his two clenched fists.

The child was truly beautiful and Lady Stuart thought she would faint when she saw him. This child, this beautiful little being who was innocently giving vent to his rage in her presence was her son—her son whom she had recovered at last after having feared that she would be separated from him forever—her son for whom she had wept, for whom she had suffered and for whom she thought she would have died.

By a spontaneous instinctive movement,

which would have appeared suspicious to an observer, she rushed up to the nurse and almost snatched him out of her arms. And then, without kissing him, she looked hard at him for a long time. But the child that she pressed to her bosom, did not resemble the one that had been stolen from her. Some months had passed since he had been taken away, and his features were modified: the vague outlines of his face had disappeared, and had been replaced by others which in their turn were destined to be effaced. Lady Stuart no longer recognized her son, and an acute sorrow, a terrible fear, assailed her. Could Detective Frépont have been mistaken: if the Masson girl, although perfectly sincere in her confession, had told the tale of an abduction precisely similar to the one of which she had been the victim, but had nothing to do with her sorrow: if, in a word, the child which she pressed to her bosom, was not her son, but the son of another woman, robbed like her, and like her in an eternal mourning?

Lady Stuart in the chaos of her mind was

nearly ready to faint, to die there in the house
in which she had hoped to experience so much
joy, and she became frightfully pale. Her dejection was too apparent to escape the notice
of the nurse. In fact she remarked it: but in
her innocence of mind attributed it to the emotion caused by her approaching maternity which
the young lady had announced to her.

"If holding the child of your friend affects
you so much, madam," she said, "how will it
be when you have one of your own?"

Did Lady Stuart hear the peasant's words?
Not at the moment. But later she recalled
them, as we recall the slightest circumstance
which has determined a crisis in our existence,
and to which, at the time of its taking place, we
paid no attention. At the moment that the
words were pronounced, they only reached her
ears as an empty sound without meaning. But
this sound recalled her to the reality of her
situation. Suddenly abandoning all painful
thought, as though moved by a specific recollection, she uncovered his right ear and having
examined it as if she were out of her mind, she

had only time to give him back to the nurse when with a loud scream she fell fainting on the tiled floor.

The man and the woman who witnessed this scene, and who did not understand it, hastened to the Countess and busied themselves in restoring her. "Poor lady," said the nurse. Then she added: "here is a woman who will make a good mother."

The man seemed to reflect: "My opinion is that all this is dubious. People are not taken ill because they kiss a friend's child."

At this moment Lady Stuart recovering from her swoon opened her eyes, and the woman signed to her husband to be silent. Both of them hung over the sick woman and waited for her to speak. But as she remained silent, and her glance wandered, the nurse tried to make her speak, thinking that this remark would bring her to her senses.

"Well, madam," said she, "are you feeling better?"

Lady Stuart then uttered the word for which she had hoped, but its effect was terrible.

"My child—" she murmured, "I want my child."

The peasants drew back frightened.

"Her child," stammered the woman, "she said 'my child!'"

"You see," replied Bernier, "that I was right. There is something queer here."

Lady Stuart who was now seated on an armchair with a bottom of plaited straw, and who had somewhat recovered her self-possesion, heard this last sentence.

"There is something queer, indeed," said she: "but there is also one truth which you ought to know: I am the mother of the child in your charge, and I am come to claim him from you."

Bernier then came forward and spoke firmly: "Madam, we don't know you. You came to us under the pretence of securing a nurse for a child, whom you are about to bring into the world, and then all of a sudden, you tell us another story, and declare that you are the mother of the child who has been entrusted to us. You must know, with all the respect that I owe you, that we are not going to give up the child to you like this, without having the proof of what you assert."

"My friend, you shall have this proof. The child you are bringing up is my son. He was stolen from the people who had charge of him as you have, and when you showed him to me, I could not recognize him, I did not recognize him. I even doubted for a moment that he belonged to me. But I remembered that my little boy, whose name is Jack--"

"Léon," corrected the man.

"Whom you call Léon," continued the Countess, "bore behind his right ear, a scar or birth-mark. This mark, your foster-child bears too, and this is what makes me certain that the child is mine."

The peasant was embarrassed: but he did not lose mistrust.

"Excuse me, madam," he replied, "if, while I fully believe that you are telling the truth, I may appear not to place faith on your words. You know that your claim must be supported by authentic proofs in order that justice may be done. Until you procure us these proofs we will not give up the child."

"You are doing rightly, my friend, and if those to whom I formerly entrusted my son had done like you, I should not have lost my son. You shall have the proofs you require, I repeat, but meantime, while we are waiting for them, I shall not separate myself from the child."

Bernier did not abate a jot of his suspicions, but the attitude of Lady Stuart impressed him, and he vaguely comprehended that the mystery which confronted him suddenly, required that he should be prudent in deeds and words. He smiled at the obstinacy of the Countess.

"Be it so madam," he concluded. "We have not a large place here but we will give you the best accommodation we can."

Then in answer to the young lady's questions regarding the details of Jack's being brought to them, he told some facts which interested her. One day a lady brought the child, saying his name was Léon, and left without giving the name of his family. This lady gave him an address in Paris to which he could write if there were occasion for it. But as he had sent two or three letters to this address and had received no reply, he did not know in face of the revelations made to him, whether they had been lost. As he had been paid a large sum of money, for the child's board, with the promise of more when it was weaned, he thought it useless to bother himself, and concluded that if there was a secret connected with the child's birth, it was forbidden him to attempt to solve it.

Lady Stuart could not refrain from tears as she listened to Bernier. So her son, her dear little Jack had been given up to good people no doubt, but to people who in time would have been unable to keep him, if the civil status of the child was demanded of them, or the payments which were an object to them ceased, which it was easy to suppose. So her son had been launched on the sea of life, like a plank cast overboard from a ship, floating on a cruel and greedy ocean.

"I will reward you," said she to Bernier, "for the care you have taken of my son, and you will not regret the trouble I am now giving you. I bless heaven that he fell into your hands. You are good people, but I shudder when I think that those who stole him, if they had willed it, could have caused him to disappear forever."

CHAPTER XIX.

The same day Lady Stuart, impatient to regain her son, wrote to the Emperor, and her letter, which was short and to the point, was like an involuntary cry of triumph and revenge.

"Sire." said she, "I am at A., near Nancy, at the house of two peasants, husband and wife, the Berniers. At their house I have found the child of whom I was robbed. But they refuse to give him up to me without proofs of my rights. I do not desire to make this proof legally, unless I am compelled to do so. I beseech your Majesty then to give orders for the immediate restoration of my son to me."

Having traced these lines, she asked Bernier to take the sealed missive to the post. The peasant, when he read the address, "To His Majesty the Emperor, at the Palace of the Tuileries," experienced a shock similar to that of a person suddenly awakened from sleep, and he began to regard Lady Stuart with less suspicion.

When the letter written by Lady Stuart reached the Tuileries the Emperor was away. As it was addressed personally to the Emperor, the chief of the cabinet and private secretary of Napoleon III., when they sorted the mail, placed it with several other envelopes on the desk of the sovereign. It was not until after some delay that the Emperor read it; and while he was sincerely pleased to hear that his mistress had at last succeeded in her search, he was also glad that the affair had ended without scandal. He telegraphed to the Prefect at Nancy ordering him to communicate with the young woman, and to respect all her wishes. Although he had attempted formerly after the occurrence at La Verrière to deny the accusations which Lady Stuart brought against the Empress, a doubt as to the Empress' part in the abduction of the child had remained in the mind of the Emperor. After a violent scene with his wife this doubt was not dispelled, and Napoleon III., who was worried by it, still wished to have it dissipated. It would have been a pleasant feeling to be perfectly certain that the Empress had had nothing to do with such a heinous action, and as he now had an opportunity for making further investigations, he decided to profit by it.

Armed with the Countess Ellen's letter, he went to the Empress and had a conversation with her in which he hoped that his suspicions would be dispelled.

She was in her room when the Emperor appeared before her.

"I am about to do violence to your feelings by speaking to you of a person whom you do not like. But pardon me. An event of such importance has just happened in connection with this person that I am compelled to communicate it to you."

The Empress, aggressive and suspicious, refrained from a sudden fit of passion.

"It is doubtless Lady Stuart of whom you are again speaking?"

The Emperor, without making a direct reply to this sentence and to avoid recriminations, answered:

"You remember that Lady Stuart suffered a dreadful misfortune by her child being stolen from her! Well, this child has been found: and as the people would not give it up to her, I have ordered the Prefect at Nancy, where she is now residing, to support her in her claims."

The Empress trembled slightly, but her face, habitually painted to hide the freckles with which it was covered, gave no clue to the state of her mind. She was silent for some moments, and then replied in an apparently indifferent and sarcastic tone:

"Truly, it is so much the better that the child should be restored to its mother. With you I rejoice at the news, if it in any way gives you satisfaction."

The Emperor understood the hostility which was concealed in her last words.

"This news gives me satisfaction for two reasons," he returned. "First of all, because a crime having been committed, it will not have the expected results: then, because your name was mixed up with the matter—of which you are aware—and there will be no further occasion for its being mentioned."

The Empress who was engaged in arranging some trinkets, turned to Napoleon III. and became violent.

"I do remember," she scolded in her harsh voice, "that you formerly insulted me by questioning me on the subject of the abduction of Lady Stuart's son. It appeared then that people dared to accuse me of taking some part in this plot: I am delighted and grieved at that accusation: I am delighted at it because I am glad that I should be thought capable of hating my enemies, even to an exaggerated extent: I am grieved at it because,—because as a matter of fact I am in no sense deserving of the plotting capacities with which I am credited."

The Emperor assumed an air of severity.

"Irony is out of place here: you should know that a scandal connected with your name, injures me more personally than it does you."

The Empress burst out:

"A scandal—you are to blame for the scandal that Lady Stuart provoked by her presence at the Tuileries, in according her outrageous privileges which I disdain even to mention! Truly, I ask myself if it can be you speaking. Yes, a scandal was caused by the act of this woman—a scandal was caused by the act of a man who had compromised himself with her—do you understand me or must I speak more plainly?"

"I understand you," replied the Emperor, "and I beg of you not to renew a scene between us which has been repeated so often already and which has nothing but jealousy for its excuse. You hate Lady Stuart as you have hated all the women who have been my mistresses—be it so. I should have thought, however, that her sorrow would have touched you, and that you would have felt some disinterested pleasure, some human joy in hearing of her mother's heart being comforted. I was mistaken. Pardon me for intruding upon your tranquillity."

Thus speaking, the Emperor left the room of his wife.

This short interview, which Napoleon III. later related to his mistress, was nearly similar to all those to which the sovereign had to submit from the Empress during his reign, with regard to his feminine relations true or imaginary. The Emperor habitually saved himself by flight from these conjugal quarrels, and this evening he did not wait for the Empress to fall into hysterics or to vent her rage by smashing various objects of furniture. He left her and returned to his apartments, bowed under a poignant grief; for the doubt that he had against his wife still remained after his discussion with her, as entire, deep and profound as before this discussion.

Few people certainly have ever thought of the Empress Eugénie in the light that she is represented here, at one time screaming at the top of her voice, or smashing in her fury anything which happened to be near her, when suffering from one of her insane attacks of passion.

This aspect is unfortunately but too true. If it is necessary to give an anecdote to prove the truth of the assertion, it will suffice to recall the scene which took place between her and Marshal Niel, when the illustrious soldier as Minister of War was actively engaged in the reorganization of the army.

It is well-known that at this time the Emperor Napoleon III. summoned, in a special council, the Marshals as well as the principal dignitaries of the Court, to consult them as to the chance of a war against Prussia and her allies. The Emperor felt that this war was inevitable, and desired that it should then be declared in place of allowing Prussia to strengthen herself, and to wage successful war against France at some future period.

But after a careful examination of our armament, it was acknowledged that we were not ready to undertake a perilous campaign, and it was resolved to increase the effective of the army, so that it might cope without too much risk, with the Prussian forces.

The Empress vehemently desired immediate action, and as she did in 1870, when she was informed that war could not be declared she had a terrible fit of passion in which she abused all who did not agree with her. People then lived at the Tuileries in a constant whirl of excitement and irritation. And one afternoon when Marshal Niel in company with the Emperor, explained to the Empress the reasons which had determined him to give up for the time the idea of an unequal strife, she in defiance of all etiquette and all reserve, behaved with great violence. Having exhausted her arguments, she seized an inkstand from the Emperor's desk and hurled it at the Marshal. The soldier who was struck on the body and covered with enormous black stains, simply bowed and retired. There was a terrible scene after his departure between the Emperor and his wife: but this quarrel no more than those which had preceded it, or those which were to follow it, had any effect in changing the character of the Empress.

This story cannot be denied. It was related by the wife of the Marshal, who is still living, to one of her friends. Marshal Niel alone could have contradicted it, but in his profound loyalty he would not have done so.

The Empress passed a week of sullenness after the discussion which she had had with her husband, but more in consequence of the rage which she felt at the news that her vengeance which she thought absolute and irremediable had been frustrated. But as she quickly reconciled herself to events good or bad which concerned her, and as her mind was incapable of dwelling for any length of time on any point no matter how important, she rapidly recovered her gaiety and carelessness, and she seemed to have forgotten the drama which had worried her for a time.

There was a reign of insane folly and unbridled dissipation at the Tuileries at that time: and in the excitement of the pleasures which the courtiers enjoyed, it was very difficult for the sovereign as well as for her intimate friends to dwell upon sorrowful subjects.

It was this extreme folly, this unbridled license selfishly oblivious of every other consideration, but the personal gratification of the hour, hurrying along in its magical and formidable whirlpool all that interfered with their voluptuous programme, that they demanded. Laughter and kisses were on all lips and in all *boudoirs*. It was in the nervous excitement of men's brains and the senses of men in the attention which they gave to it, that none perceived that in the imperial sky, till then serene, clouds were gathering fraught with threatening lightnings, driven along by a violent tempest, accompanied by prophetic growlings. The year 1869 died away in a sort of unacknowledged convulsion and with it the Empire or rather the clan of courtiers who were incarnated with it were joyously dying away with it. Everything at this time, in the streets of Paris, in the Provinces and abroad should have imposed silence on the laughing crowds. But their joyful egoism was on too steep an incline to allow of its return, and all men and women were hurrying to the abyss with the frightful but superb intoxication of demi-gods, who do not realize that their cult is a thing of the past. The courtiers of the Second Empire were marvellous voluptuaries, who can, not unreasonably be compared with the ancient patricians, who loved to die amid the sleepy perfume of roses and in the exhausting fever of their *amours*.

CHAPTER XX.

It was during this time of cynical intoxication, of this unacknowledged alarm that Lady Stuart returned to Paris with her son.

Detective Frépont was there faithful to his trust, and with some difficulty maintaining control of Miss Masson. As soon as she saw Lady Stuart the young woman thought that her captivity was over and made a joyful movement. But she did not allow for the hatred of the woman she had made to suffer, and at the first words she addressed to her she was cruelly undeceived.

"I bring back my son," said Lady Stuart to her, "not owing to your kindness or your confession, but owing to the fear of the reprisals, which you deserved. The other day in my grief I would have tortured you with pleasure; to-day in my happiness I will not do you any harm, but I ask myself if I ought, as you wish, to set you free, to let you out of my house without having suffered some expiation. What shall I do with you? What punishment shall I impose? I don't know. But, meantime, I have come to a resolution concerning you,—I shall keep you, you belong to me."

This speech filled the mind of the young girl with fear. Despairing of obtaining any hope of deliverance from Lady Stuart, she turned to Detective Frépront to beg him to intercede for her in regard to her fate.

"You are imprisoning me," she declared, "for which, later, you will have to account to the Courts. What is wanted of me? Whether voluntarily or by force I have aided in the recovery of the child. Henceforth I have nothing more to do with the mother. What do these enigmatical words mean that she has uttered? She is not going to kill me I suppose."

Frépont patted her shoulder good-naturedly. "Lady Stuart has not revealed her plans to me," he said, " but I think I can affirm that she will not embarrass herself with you for very long. Be patient then: it is best : as to legal proceedings, give up the idea at once ; that will be better still."

"If I tell, however, people would be obliged to listen to me."

"No, my girl, no, they would not listen to you."

"And why, if you please?"

The detective began to laugh.

"You ask why? Truly you ought to know the profession better. Don't you know that we ought never to 'tell,' because in doing so we would often compromise personages who do not allow themselves to be compromised. And then——"

"And then? ——"

"There are corks for whistles which make too much noise."

Martha Masson trembled. This vulgar phrase brought up before her eyes a mysterious force, against which the imprudent or the daring would be crushed, and always fatally.

She made no reply, bent her head and appeared to accept the resignation which she was advised to do.

The morning after her return to Paris, Lady Stuart sent a few hasty lines to the Emperor to thank him for his intervention, and to give him an account of what had happened.

Napoleon III. soon sent M. Hyrvoix to her in order to hold a conversation with her and know her intentions for the future, and her attitude henceforth as regards the Tuileries.

But all the finesse of the police agent was foiled by the reticence of Lady Stuart. She received him graciously but told him nothing. He was forced to retire without having been able to elicit a word from her, relative to the mission with which he was charged. The Countess simply expressed to him her absolute determination not to confide in any one but the Emperor, and M. Hyrvoix in place of bearing to his master a conclusive answer, was the bearer only to him of a request from the young lady for an interview.

In spite of the many preoccupations which engaged the Emperor at that time; in spite of the uneasinesses which disquieted him, Lady Stuart always occupied his thoughts, and he was obliged to confess that the passion with which she had inspired in him was not dead.

As much then, with the hope of averting another scandal, as to see his mistress again, he yielded to her request.

When he again saw the women whom he had loved so profoundly, and with whom he had spent so many rapturous hours, the Emperor forgot the events which had estranged her from him and was really moved.

He seized her hands, kissed her tenderly, and remained silent for a moment in the close embrace by which his caress was returned. The Countess was as much moved as was the Emperor, and she smiled at the expression of his attachment, as one smiles at something dear of which one has been deprived for a long time and has had no hope of ever again enjoying. Notwithstanding this exchange of caresses, the Emperor desired to know the details of the adventure, which had resulted so happily for the young woman, and she gave him an account of what she had undergone, without omitting a single detail.

While she was speaking the Emperor was thoughtful, as if buried in deep reflections, and only roused himself from his preoccupation to raise his hands to heaven, with a gesture, which at this moment perhaps signified many things which he could not reveal.

"I rejoiced with you," he said to her at last, "at the favorable result of your search. You have your son now: never leave him again."

Lady Stuart looked fixedly at her imperial visitor. Suddenly she asked him:

"Well, sire, do you think now that you know the whole story of the abduction, that I was wrong when I affirmed to you—"

Napoleon guessed what she was about to say and interrupted her.

"You have recovered your happiness. Do not accuse any one any more."

"Since you elude my question, sire, I will not repeat it: but in eluding a question do we not recognize the truth of it,—do we not acknowledge its legitimacy?"

"In pity, madam, do not torture me, and speak no more to me of this intrigue. The Empress, do not forget it, ought not to have been mixed up with the La Verrière plot. As to my personal feeling about all these matters, I do not wish to conceal it: there are people at the Tuileries who serve me badly in their desire to be agreeable to the Empress. Every day I notice around me compromising circumstances, which cause me uneasiness, and which throw discredit on my name and authority. We no longer live in a period when the residence of a monarch is exempt from public gaze. The liberty which I have given to the Press takes advantage of the curiosity of the public and it is hostile to me. How is it that those who pretend to love me do not understand that they are playing the game of my worst enemies, when they give their support and countenance to scandal, no matter from what source, whatever the hand which directs it, whatever the caprice which allows it?"

The Countess listened to the Emperor attentively, and heard his complaints with astonishment.

"One word from you, sire, would be sufficient to put a stop to this anarchy at the Tuileries."

Napoleon III. as he walked up to the young woman replied:

"One word from me: do you think, madam that a word from me would have weight with the coteries, which are formed and which disturb the Château? You are mistaken. I have spoken this word and have repeated it, but it was not listened to. Ah! there are times when I am tempted to admit—a thing, however, which seems to me impossible—where I am tempted to admit that not one of those around me, really loves me; that none of those who bow before me, fear me; that none of those whom I support like parasites—has any care for my happiness, for the future of my dynasty. All these men and women who share the pleasure which I procure for them, I begin to believe look upon me only as the caterer to their pleasures, and justify their egoism, by what they call—I have it on good authority my dream."

The Emperor was again silent: then he went on with a louder voice than usual:

" They are fools—they are fools—they are perhaps miserable creatures—they rely too much upon my kindness. But let them beware the day will come when I will make them return to their duty—or I will banish them—"

Lady Stuart was far from expecting this scene, in which the sovereign appeared as if in spite of himself to pour out the full extent of his bitterness, to show that he was not blind to the eccentricities, and the responsibilities, which the frequenters of the Tuileries were accumulating under the protection of his name.

She could not restrain an exclamation:

"Is it true, sire, that this heart-rending picture which you draw of your house is correct?

Is it true that your goodness has only had the result of causing to spring up around you, selfishness and hypocrisy?"

"That is true, madam. However, I ought not to be unjust in the sorrow which I am suffering. I am loved at the Tuileries by Lepic and two or three other brave hearts, who do not enjoy the better part of the pleasures at the Château. I am also loved—you will laugh, madam—by my servants, and I mean by servants the personal attendants at the Palace. Apart from these, I am surrounded by falsities and interested baseness."

And the Emperor wore an air of unspeakable discouragement, sadness and disgust:

"Ah! madam, if you knew!"

Then he added:

"When evil days come, then you will see them all—these courtiers who are dependent on my life, disperse and forget me."

The young woman endeavored to dispel the melancholy of the sovereign, but he commanded silence with a gesture, and concluded:

"I ask your pardon—I am worrying you,

and am allowing myself to be carried away in your presence, because I know that you are my friend, to talk of things aloud, regarding which I ought, perhaps, to be silent. Let us not speak any more of these things, and let me know rather what you now propose to do?"

Lady Stuart smiled.

"M. Hyrvoix has already asked me that question, sire, and I refused to answer him. From you, I will not conceal that it is my intention to continue to live in Paris, and not to live the life of a recluse any longer. I love society and since the Tuileries are closed to me, I hope to create distractions for myself elsewhere."

The Emperor caressed his moustache.

"I understand your desire. You can no longer content yourself with a life of isolation. But the world is dangerous for those who have a history. Be prudent, madam."

"The world is dangerous and wicked only for those who wish it to rule them. I will take much from it, sire, but be assured that I will give it nothing."

Napoleon III. came and seated himself beside the Countess.

"And I, what shall I be to you in all this?" he murmured with the charming timidity which was customary with him when with women for whom he entertained a serious passion : you too will forget me, and will swell the number of those who are indifferent to me."

The young woman said caressingly:

"You, sire, will be for me to-morrow what you were yesterday, before our cruel separation: I shall not forget you in my happiness, since I remembered you in my grief."

A kiss fell on Lady Stuart's hand and was followed by a murmuring.

The Emperor, again conquered by the beauty of his mistress, allowed himself to be carried away by her seductive arts, and she herself was triumphant for she had feared that henceforth her charms might be powerless over the sovereign, whereas she now felt herself a gainer by this illusion of a love, which, in the real sense of the word, she had never felt. This evening brought her the first minutes of true happiness, that she had tasted since the tragic events which had plunged her in mourning.

When the sovereign was about to leave her, he seemed suddenly anxious, and referring to the story she had told him of the abduction, he said to her:

"You must not keep as a prisoner any longer the young woman of whom you spoke to me, who was an accomplice in the abduction of your son. Let her return home. I assure you that you will have nothing to fear from her henceforth."

At the mention of the name of Miss Masson, Lady Stuart made an angry movement.

"Sire, you ask from me the sacrifice of my hate."

"Make this sacrifice for me."

"Granted. One cannot refuse a favor to one who grants so many. To-morrow the girl shall be free."

The Emperor thanked his mistress for her obedience to his wish: then he left the hotel followed at a distance by the detectives who guarded his nocturnal promenade and who had calmly paced the sidewalk while they awaited him.

CHAPTER XXI.

THE MURDER OF MARTHA MASSON.

SOME days after the Emperor's visit to Lady Stuart, the detective Frépont called on the young lady, in much emotion.

" Well, my good Frépont, what has happened? You look upset."

The detective with an impressive gesture, replied :

" Ah ! madam, I should think I am upset ! A thing has just happened—an extraordinary thing."

Lady Stuart gave a short, dry laugh.

" Come, tell me this thing, Frépont. But after what has happened to me, I doubt if I shall be astonished no matter how extraordinary it may be."

The detective replied:

"It concerns Martha Masson, madam."

"Martha Masson? This girl does not interest me any more."

"You will be interested, madam."

"What do you mean?"

"She is dead!"

Lady Stuart started.

"She is dead!"

"It is just as I have the honor to announce to you. Her body was found in the Seine this morning, near Neuilly."

The young woman looked at the detective.

"Heaven has punished her crime. I do not pity her, I can't pity her: she did me too much harm."

Then bethinking herself:

"But you are thinking a lot of things which you dare not confess to me—I believe you think that it is I who have caused the assassination of this girl to avenge myself?"

The detective shook his head negatively, and lowering his voice:

"I know, madam, that you had no hand in

the death of Martha Masson ; but on the other hand, I know the story of her suicide, for the newspapers will tell you that Martha Masson was killed."

Lady Stuart who was puzzled, motioned the detective to a seat.

"You were right, Frépont, you have interested me. Sit down there and tell me the story."

The detective seated himself facing the young woman, and began his tale.

"I thought nothing, madam, when the other day you told me all of a sudden, that you had given up the idea of reprisals against Martha Masson. But I recalled the serious accusation that you had formerly brought against a certain high personage, on whose instigation this girl acted, according to you, and I thought that if this accusation was really founded, the discovery of the child would be followed by some incident. Miss Masson unmasked by you, living and free, although she had only an imperfect knowledge of the secret of the drama, in which she had played a part, was dangerous for those who had employed her. If she ever made up her mind to talk, how would it be possible to silence her? She held in her hands a scandal which might be revealed at any time. And in all ages and in all countries and under all governments, it is a tradition madam, to get rid of a troublesome person.

Miss Masson being a disquieting personality, henceforth, I was sure that her matter would not end there. As I am not 'working' now, I have been amusing myself by watching her and following her, and have been well repaid for the pains I took on her account. Hear me, madam, and you will not laugh, I swear. Yesterday night, I was watching in front of the house of Miss Masson, when a man came out with her and went towards the Champs-Elysées in company with her. There, like a lover, he called a cab and was driven towards L'Etoile. I followed them to the bridge of Neuilly. There, the man and Miss Masson again alighted and paid the driver, and went on their way arm-in-arm along the banks of the Seine which lead to St. James. Without losing sight of the man and the girl, I kept on their track. They walked thus for about a kilomètre. Then the man stopped —then, madam, oh ! then, I saw a horrible thing !

The unfortunate girl believing surely that she was in good luck, and that she was going to some villa belonging to her companion, for the man had seized her as if to embrace her and she submitted to him sweetly and gently. He did embrace her in fact ; then suddenly seizing her by the waist, he threw her violently from him. The poor girl stumbled on the bank which is perpendicular, or very nearly so, at that spot, lost her balance, gave a loud scream, a scream which I shall always hear, and disappeared under the water. There was a muffled splash like the beating of wet linen, and all was still again. The gentleman stood motionless leaning over the Seine, remained a good half-hour, passing and repassing the scene of the crime. Then certain that nothing could betray him, that his task was accomplished, he quietly returned to Paris, his hands in his pockets. for it was rather cold.

"If I had arrested him, he would have been

astonished: but I was not there to meddle with his plans, and his business did not concern me."

And the detective philosophically added, with the tone of a man accustomed to all kinds of sights which are not to be talked about:

" Everyone has his own affairs in life, isn't it so ? "

Then he concluded:

" That is what I saw, madam. Wasn't it worth the trouble of telling you ? "

The young woman had listened anxiously to the recital of the detective. When he spoke, she did not answer him, and seemed at first to be buried in deep thought. But she returned to the reality of events.

" Certainly, my dear Frépont, this new drama deserved to be related to me."

And she murmured : " I was asked to give her liberty to this unhappy woman, and to promise that I would not revenge myself on her. It would have been better for her if I had made her undergo some punishment. I would not have killed her and should have been content to exile her from Paris."

Then with a laugh:

"It was quite right to tell me of this affair, Frépont, but I advise you not to spread this adventure."

The detective bowed and extended his hand as if to take an oath.

"Be reassured on my account, madam. It would cost me more than I should like if I did not hold my tongue about this affair. No matter how much I may wish it, I shall not attempt to recognize the man of the drowning. It is well to hunt birds like him at a distance. If one attempts to put one's hand in their nest, it gets pecked."

When the detective had left, the Countess commenced to meditate on the fate of the pretty girl who had made her suffer so much.

"Decidedly," she thought, "I am not without pity for this unhappy girl. An instrument always ready for crime, this woman was destined to disappear by a crime. I pronounced her condemnation when I granted the Emperor his favor the other evening. The Emperor is good but the extreme measure he has taken astonishes me. The Emperor is good, yes but on this occasion, reasons of State bound him, and if Miss Masson lived, it was likely that at some indefinite period the whole intrigue of La Verrière would be revealed publicly, the Empress compromised, and my peace endangered by blackmail. The girl had to die. A State reason, after all, is not such a bad invention for those who benefit by its enforcement."

Having finished her meditations, Lady Stuart went to her son whom she found in charge of his guardian. She took him in her arms and covered him with kisses as if he had escaped some imaginary danger: and as it was a clear and fine day, she took him around the lake in the Bois de Boulogne.

CHAPTER XXII.

In the renewal of her intimacy with the Emperor, Lady Stuart was clever enough to avoid all allusion to the disappearance of Martha Masson, and did not even recall the memories of the La Verrière drama. The interest or rather the curiosity which the tragic tale of Detective Frépont had excited in her had been succeeded by an absolute indifference to the fate of the unfortunate member of the *demi-monde*, and aside from that in the affection which she entertained for her son, in the active surveillance which she exercised over him and in the proud satisfaction which she felt in the undiminished affection of the Emperor, she enjoyed an undisturbed joy, and contented herself with being simply happy.

As she had told the Emperor, she had re-entered society--having thrown her house open to certain friends—to women of fashion belonging to the foreign colony, and to political men principally, and she seemed by the quietness of her existence, to have re-established herself in the influence which her name and her beauty formerly exercised, and to have forgotten the tears which she had shed.

All of a sudden—it was then in the month

of July 1870—a lamentable rumor interrupted the even tenor of her life. Without any preparation for the sad surprise, war was declared between France and Prussia and Lady Stuart with her perspicacity, and knowing the dangers which menaced the Emperor, foresaw that from this war would result the upheaval of all those things which had dazzled the world, of the state of affairs which the careless had thought eternal, beyond all human vicissitudes, and all political complications. Disasters followed one another with bewildering rapidity, and the young woman realized that all was over for her and the Emperor in the country over which he had ruled.

She went to the English Embassy, saw Lord Lyons, who confirmed her apprehensions, and she no longer doubted that the Empire would be destroyed, as much from the defeat of her armies, as by the powerful popular outcry raised against it, and which was already passing over the Tuileries like a whirlwind.

Lady Stuart without being as much enamored of the Emperor Napoleon as he was of her, had a sincere affection for him, because she knew he was a good man, because he was unhappy in his conjugal relations, as well as in the material and moral management of his official household, owing to the fools and the follies, which, under favor of his inexhaustible indulgence, caused his unpopularity. She therefore experienced a real and terrible grief and heartfelt despair at seeing the Emperor embark in this adventurous and formidable enterprise.

However, she had not been able entirely to lose sight of the fact that in the strife that she had waged against her to whom she attributed all her grief, she had only obtained a semi-satisfaction and an incomplete revenge, and if she feared that the Emperor might fall in the bloody abyss of war, she could not refrain from thinking that the Empress would fall with him, and that this war which frightened her offered her also the absolute vengeance for which she wished and which she had been obliged to renounce. Fate was going to give her reprisals in comparison with which those for which she had wished were commonplace, and she smiled and she contemplated Fate like an invisible phantom, intervening in the life of mankind, with the supreme authority of an officer of justice.

The Emperor at the time ill and worn-out, was taking his summer vacation with the Court at St. Cloud. As she had not seen him for several days she wrote to him to express her fears, and to testify her solicitude for him in his present critical position. She was aware that one woman, the Countess de Mercy-Argenteau, had consoled him somewhat during the last few months of her intimacy with the Emperor, if not from his passion for her, at least by the attentions to which she had accustomed him: but she felt no anger against the Emperor for his inconstancy: she understood too well the temptations by which he was surrounded not to excuse him; and seeing that, as a matter of fact, he had remained attached to her, she was desirous that her affectionate words should console him in the dire griefs which overwhelmed him.

" You are about to place yourself at the head

of your army, sire," she said to him, "and I weep at the perils which you are about to encounter. I do not dare under the serious circumstances which are convulsing the world, to ask you to grant me an opportunity of saying adieu to you. Shall we see one another again? God, alone, whom I pray to protect you, can answer this question. You have always been dear to me: you are still dearer to me when I feel that you are in danger."

The unhappy sovereign, whose every minute was then devoted to the preparations for the campaign, was moved when he received her letter. When he answered her he excused himself for not having the leisure to see her before his departure, thanked her for her friendly words and assured her that he would never forget her. His letter was short, somewhat disjointed and almost illegible. He had evidently written her under the influence of sorrowful presentiments.

At this time, when so many tragical events were happening and were announced at the Court of St. Cloud, the men and women forming the imperial suite concerned themselves but little, as I have already demonstrated in preceding works, about the situation of the Emperor and the country.

The frequenters of the Tuileries continued to live well, laugh, make love, making an occasional halt when they were breathless with their pleasures, to shout, "*A Berlin!*" but without pity for the profound sadness of the Emperor, without respect for his wish to avoid a conflict between France and Prussia. People amused themselves at the Court at this time confronted with a vision of death as they had formerly done when the future was smiling.

They played games, told stories as they gaily walked about, but utterly refused to discuss the gravity of events, or even to talk about them.

One of the gallants at the Court one day uttered a typical "*mot*" on this subject. When an officer of the palace dared to express before him a sorrowful doubt as to the issue of the campaign, he disdainfully exclaimed:

"Truly, my dear fellow, you are a nuisance, and if we were to listen to you there would be

an end to pleasure. The issue of the campaign
-the issue of the campaign, well, isn't that
settled,—we are going to make love to the
women of Berlin, and that will be charming!"

A witness of the heart-rending spectacle
which the Court presented in 1870, reports that
the Empress, no more than the courtiers, refrained from the affectation of a careless gaiety.
She amused herself by telling stories and they
were not a little doubtful in character.

There is another fact still more characteristic
and which incontestably proves the criminal indifference of the friends of the imperial family.
The same day that the news of the defeat at
Wissembourg, was received at the Court, some
fried gudgeons were being served at table.
And what do you suppose was the subject of
conversation during the repast? It was
gudgeons. This assertion may appear to be a
senseless exaggeration: but it is a fact. It
was M. de Cossé-Brisac who started the conversation on this important subject, in comparison with which the poor soldiers mowed
down and conquered on the frontier, doubtless

had no interest for all these fools. M. de Cossé-Brisac was afraid of eating gudgeons if they were spawned in the Seine, because of the pollution of the river. Then each one had something to say on the more or less hygienic condition of the fry: and as it was known that the fish had been caught in the Seine, no one dared touch them. While these events were happening at St. Cloud, while the courtiers were standing terrified before a plate of fried gudgeons, unfortunate men who faced the *mitrailleuse* were falling mutilated, and the Emperor erring and unhappy bestrode in a fantastic gallop—a horse urged on by Disaster.

Lady Stuart was well avenged. Misfortune had overtaken the Empire,—and the Empress, her rival of the year before,—the Empress who had banished her from the Tuileries, who had tortured her. -having returned to Paris was anxiously awaiting the last and supreme hour of her ruin.

In fact there was no longer room for doubt: the Empire was about to disappear in the smoke of battle, as well as in the anger of the masses, who in the shadow of the suburbs, were seething and hurling imprecations against it.

Marshal Ma-Mahon having been vanquished at Worth, had retreated on Chalons, where the Emperor had met him.

Lady Stuart, although she experienced a pitiless satisfaction at the gradual downfall of the Empress, was profoundly afflicted at the thought of the unfortunate Emperor fleeing from camp to camp, under the blows of an implacable destiny.

She had a terribly sad dream of him who had been her lover: she saw him bowed down beneath the weight of his misfortunes, which he had not deserved, crouching under the cruel hand of a fate towards which he had been sorrowfully driven: she saw him isolated, feverish, like an unfortunate creature repulsed by all, clinging to his misfortunes even to try and draw some hope from them, and she told herself that he was hers, that it was her duty, having derived happiness from him, to offer him consolation, and the infinite and comforting tenderness of a woman—that tenderness which loving lips understand how to administer to an agonized heart and from which it draws a last and delicious sensation of life as it dies.

Without thinking of the obstacles which she would encounter, or rather without being willing to admit these obstacles, she resolved to leave for Chalons and see the Emperor.

CHAPTER XXIII.

When Napoleon III. unsealed the note in which she informed him of her presence near him, and in which she begged him to receive her, he was much moved. The affection that this woman showed him who had only been his mistress, and who had suffered on his account—this spontaneous affection compared with the indifference of those he had left at Paris, of those whom he had in the time of his power and good fortune, gorged with gold and love, touched him profoundly.

He desired that Lady Stuart should come to him as soon as possible, and he sent an officer of artillery to carry her his summons.

When she appeared in his presence she found him surrounded by several generals, who discreetly retired at her approach.

Then the unhappy sovereign, mournful, exhausted, with humid eyes and trembling hands, advanced to Lady Stuart, and without a word and with a gesture of utter despair, he opened his arms and held them extended towards her.

The Countess Ellen who had turned very pale in presence of this supreme affliction, rushed to the Emperor, seized one of his trembling hands and raised it to her lips. But Napoleon III. drew her to him, and letting his head fall on her shoulder, like a child in trouble, drew a long sigh. Then he uttered words of complaint:

"My friend, my poor friend ——"

Lady Stuart tried to console him, to respond to his lamentation, by some words of hope, but the Emperor having seated himself and having placed her by his side, shook his head sadly:

"No," said he, "all is finished: we are conquered, and I am nothing but a plank tossed in a storm."

And pointing to heaven, he murmured:

"My star is no longer in the ascendant, you know it—that star that the world thought was faithful to me and in which I gloried when I was happy."

The young woman whom the sorrow and the discouragement of Napoleon III. overwhelmed, ceased all consolation.

"Ah! sire," she cried, "why did you desire this war, why did you wish to add an uncertain satisfaction to that which was already assured to you?"

The Emperor who at the time was suffering much physically, was sallow and as if quite overcome by the misfortune which tortured him. When he heard these words, however, he recovered himself and looked fixedly at his friend.

"You think," he said, "like all the world that I wished for this atrocious war which is ruining France, and which will cost me my throne, perhaps——"

The young woman remained silent and waited for the Emperor to explain himself. He guessed the question which she dared not formulate, and replied :

"I did not wish the war—I did all I could to avoid it. I thought and still think that the sudden difference which arose between France and Prussia could be peacefully adjusted. But they rendered all arrangement between the two countries impossible, and war became inevitable owing to complications, intrigues, misunderstandings, imprudences, of which I yet know nothing and which mocked at my wishes in the dark."

Lady Stuart, who was stupefied, uttered an involuntary exclamation :

"How, sire, you did not wish for war and you signed the declaration of it!"

The Emperor seized the young woman's arm with a tight grasp.

"You don't know—you can't know—I declared war because I was not permitted to oppose it."

"But who around you, sire, had sufficient

authority, sufficient infernal ingenuity, to force you into an undertaking which you did not approve?"

Napoleon III. moved his lips, as if about to speak. But he simply raised his hands, which he let fall again on his knees, and stammered:

"I cannot answer your question, madam."

There was silence for a moment and the Emperor and his mistress gazed at one another, and seemed to exchange the same thought which it was forbidden them to express. Then the Emperor spoke and his innate fatalism plainly revealed itself:

"Whether I desired the war or whether it was forced upon me by a superior power to mine, the war exists, and it would be puerile to recriminate. It was to be without doubt, and all that I could have attempted to obviate it would have been useless. The days of men, their joys as well as their sorrows are counted, and none can lessen or augment the number. My happiness is at an end, and my sorrow begins. Where will this misfortune lead me? Will it be but fleeting, and will the magic star, of which I spoke but now, reappear for me in heaven? A Calvary confronts me: I think I shall climb it to the summit: it is a mysterious and undeniable fact which presents itself in the lives of men: having been given in the evolution of humanity unmingled joy and of long duration, the hour comes when this joy dies to give place to sorrow. My happiness, or rather the happiness of those who surrounded me, has existed too long, and the time when all happiness is paid for by tears, has come for me."

The Emperor paused and a deep melancholy took possession of him.

"Only," he resumed, "fate is unjust to me, under the present circumstances: I am paying a higher tribute than others, more than those whose follies I have so often deplored, and who are in reality its debtors."

Lady Stuart much moved and very pale, listened to the Emperor, without being able to find a word to dispel this lamentable sadness. She desired, however, to reply to him.

"What are you going to do, sire?" she asked.

" All, even the impossible, to save France."

" What do you hope for—a victory—a great and early victory ? "

Napoleon III. with a slow and prophetic accent, uttered this sentence :

" I hope for nothing."

The young woman uttered a cry.

" Sire, you are desperate and wish to die."

" A man, madam, rarely wishes to die. But there are sometimes cases where he must think of death."

And as the Countess Ellen with a sudden and long-continued burst of tears, was about to protest, he stopped her and affectionately and tenderly careful of her feelings, said :

" Let us forget our grief for a time and talk rather of yourself. You will suffer from the sorrows which are crushing me, and who knows, will perhaps curse my memory ? "

Lady Stuart sincerely revolted at these words and there was some contempt in her voice.

" I figured too little, sire, among the courtiers of the Tuileries to be either forgetful or ungrateful. I shall always remember you and I shall love you in misfortune, as I have loved you when you were prosperous."

The Emperor was moved.

"I believe you," said he, "I believe you. You have always been good to me even when you were angry, and certain ill-founded suspicions agitated your mind, and provoked your resentment against my relatives. I thank you for all the affection you have lavished on me. I thank you for having come here to console me."

As the young woman redoubled her sobs, he added, sorrowfully :

"Alas! we are about to part forever, perhaps—Ah! poor friend, poor friend, how sad is our adieu."

This interview was indeed to be the last that Lady Stuart had with the Emperor. She never again saw him after the war, in his exile, and she only reappeared at his coffin to weep for him.

As she was about to take leave of Napoleon III., he rose and going to his campaign outfit, he said :

"I wish that you should carry away a souvenir of myself,—of this interview."

And he offered her a beautiful coffee cup of precious metal which the Countess Ellen has religiously preserved, which she shows to her intimate friends carefully locked in a glass case, in her *salon*.

CHAPTER XXIV.

RETURNING to Paris she rejoined her son: and in the increasing disturbances she waited for an unexpected turn of fortune to happen to relieve her anxiety for the fate of Napoleon III.

But fate seemed to take a tragic pleasure in mutilating the Empire, and each day brought the world news of a new defeat of the French armies.

It soon became evident that some drama arising from the turbulence of the Parisians, would be added to that which was being enacted on the fields of battle, and Lady Stuart who was alarmed not for herself, but for her child, at the thought of a popular outbreak, resolved to leave Paris.

When the catastrophe of Sedan was announced, she had packed her trunks, closed her house and was living at the hotel Meurice, in the Rue de Rivoli.

It was the afternoon of the 4th September 1870. Lady Stuart had decided to go to Italy, there to await the crisis which nearly the whole of Europe was then undergoing, and she was engaged prior to departure on the very evening of this famous day in arranging her effects, when noises suddenly rising from the street made her tremble.

She went to the window of her room while little Jack who was then two years of age, trotted here and there among the disorder of her trunks, and she beheld a scene that she will never forget.

An immense multitude, bands of men, women and children loomed like the angry sea at a distance, in the Place de la Concorde, and was advancing towards the Tuileries with terrible shouts.

It was the death of the Second Empire which the People was chanting in a terrible *De Profundis:* it was the gigantic death-note of the Second Empire, which the human masses yelled, savage, destroying, delirious with an exasperated high-strung patriotism: and Lady Stuart with a prompt conception of affairs understood all the superb grandeur as well as the awful horror which characterized this conquered people whom a vision of victories had made an executioner.

The mob entering the garden of the Château, passed like an animated water-spout under her window, and she contemplated it with fear as well as with involuntary admiration.

Then she was seized with a singular feeling; she had a baleful vision of the events which were to take place at the Tuileries behind those balconies and windows towards which the mob was resolutely advancing.

She beheld a woman whom she detested— she had a vision of the Empress, alarmed, fleeing before the tumult, and in her turn cast forth from the palace where she had reigned: she felt all the intense feeling of her old hate revive, and she told herself that destiny was avenging her at this time, more than she could ever have avenged herself for the wrong done her: she told herself that destiny, inciting these infuriated men and women to an attack on the palace in a spirit of patriotic reprisals, realized for her the supreme and delicious accompaniment of a revenge for her sufferings.

In the room little Jack played with the clothes which littered the floor, and in the street men in greater and never-ceasing numbers, with bare arms, in blouses or in coats, with gleaming, bloodshot eyes, pulled down the imperial emblems and cast the eagles in the gutter.

Lady Stuart alarmed at the fury which urged these men on, with a bound reached her son, took him in her arms, and returning with him to the window of her room, she showed him the masses of people, the dismembered eagles, the Tuileries sad and deserted, and then caus ing the little child to clap his hands in applause, she uttered a savage, strident triumphant cry:

"Look, little one at all these men, at all these things—we are being avenged!"

* * * * * * *

As we said at the beginning of these pages, Lady Stuart returned to France after the war, and took up her residence in Paris. She subsequently became the friend of the Duke of Edinburgh, who visited her secretly when he went to Paris, and by him she had two sons.

Her son Jack, the son of the Emperor Napoleon III., is now one of the most distinguished officers in the British army.

FINIS.

COPYRIGHT AND MISCELLANEOUS PUBLICATIONS ISSUED BY J. SELWIN TAIT & SONS

What One Woman Thinks.

ESSAYS OF HARYOT HOLT CAHOON. With frontispiece Edited by CYNTHIA M. WESTOVER. 12mo, cloth, gilt top, $1.25.

A series of brilliant essays which no household should be without. The charm of this gifted author's personality is perceptible in every line.

"It is because these various essays are so unstudied, are so natural, and have nothing foreign in their sentiment that one likes them so well. An essentially American woman is here writing for us."—*New York Times*.

"These essays are a judicious combination of thought and expression. They treat of homely matters chiefly, and reveal a true woman. . . . The collaboration is a pleasing success, both from a literary and moral point of view."
—*The Churchman*.

"This series of brilliant essays make a volume of intense interest, dealing both with people and things. The marked personality of this gifted author is shown throughout the book; clear-cut versatility and depth of thought are constantly apparent. . . . Everybody should read these essays."—*Boston Times*.

"The sketches are to be commended for their concise and pleasant manner of saying what is to be said directly and without unnecessary circumlocution. They are pointed, witty, and in most cases just. . . . One of the best is an early one, 'What Shall I Say to Peggy?'"—*Chicago Times*.

"You cannot read beyond page seven without a touch of the throat paralysis that is akin to tears. . . . 'Infinite riches in a little room.'"
—*New York Telegram*.

Tavistock Tales.

By GILBERT PARKER, author of 'The Chief Factor," etc., and others. Illustrated. 12mo, cloth, $1.25. Paper, 50c.

Mr. Gilbert Parker's talent is very conspicuous in this work, and the same may be said of the other authors. Each story rivals the other in dramatic force and skill in treatment. No better book for the holidays can be imagined

TAVISTOCK TALES—*Continued.*

"The best of taste has been shown in the selection of these stories. . . . We know of few short stories more impressive than Gilbert Parker's 'The March of the White Guard.'"—*New York Times.*

"The book is a charming one, and it is most attractively illustrated, by six competent artists, in black and white."—*Boston Beacon.*

"A volume full of power and pathos, dealing with great struggles in the lives of mankind, they have the virtue of being intensely human. . . . Together they form a delectable feast of pleasing variety."—*Public Opinion.*

"One of the most entertaining volumes of short stories of the season, because of their variety and strength. . . . 'The March of the White Guard' is by far the strongest and most dramatic."—*Boston Times.*

"A book that cannot be too highly commended."
—*Commercial Bulletin*, Minneapolis.

"It will make a delightful and ornamental addition to any family library, especially where the family contains young people."—*Kansas City Journal.*

"A cool, refreshing volume for summer reading is 'Tavistock Tales.' . . . We can strongly recommend it."—*Detroit Free Press.*

Told by the Colonel.

By W. L. ALDEN. Illustrated. 12mo, cloth, $1.25. Paper, 50c.

"The Colonel's repertory is of the funniest, and the most absurd things are given in the gravest manner, and it is the amusing contrast, the jumble of things plausible and impossible, that catches hold of the listeners. No human being ever could work the qualifying adjective as does Mr. Alden."—*New York Times.*

"His humor is clean and enjoyable."—*Boston Times.*

"Everyone will enjoy the sketches, which are sure to provoke a hearty laugh."
—*Boston Courier.*

"The stories have considerable breadth. Former readers of the *New York Times* who revelled in the humor of W. L. Alden will hail the appearance of this new volume."—*Chicago Tribune.*

"Here's a good antidote for the blues. If a sick or melancholy person should secure a copy he would soon be a cured man."—*Burlington Hawk Eye.*

"Mr. Alden's humor produces the happy effect of good wine."
—*Philadelphia Inquirer.*

"The whole will serve very well as a prescription for any one suffering with an attack of the blues."—*San Francisco Morning Call.*

"The stories abound in humorous situations, quaint characters, and bright witticisms. The author's fertile fancy is happily combined with a terse and forcible style."—*Outing.*

"The stories are really funny, not mere attempts in that direction. The illustrations are also well done and increase in no small degree the amusement to be derived from the book."—*Boston Herald.*

"Catchy enough to interest a child, with an undercurrent satirical moral deep enough for the grandest statesman."—*Harrisburg Telegram.*

"The author of 'The Adventures of Jimmy Brown,' who was a naughty boy always getting into trouble, . . . has the gift of fastening our attention and amusing us."—*Detroit Free Press.*

"Written in a particularly bright and lively style, and makes most excellent reading."—*New Orleans Picayune.*

"Full of bright, clean humor and sharp sarcasm."—*St. Louis Post Dispatch.*

"In one story, 'Thompson's Tombstone,' there is a drollery worthy of Mark Twain."—*Evening Bulletin*, Philadelphia.

"Mr. Alden is a born humorist, and his book ought to heighten the joy of the nations."—*N. Y. Recorder.*

"Stories like these of Mr. Alden's affect the mental appetite after the manner of a piquant sauce. . . . The 'ridiculous' power of the whole list of stories is wonderful."—*Boston Ideas.*

At the Rising of the Moon.

By FRANK MATHEW. Illustrated by Fred. Pegram and A. S. Boyd. 12mo, cloth, $1.25.

"'At the Rising of the Moon' is but a little volume, and its stories are brief and not many, but the very heart of Ireland beats in them. One by one the various national types appear; it is a motley company, but every figure abounds in character, and Mr. Mathew, whether by imitation or by grace of similar natural gift, makes each one as effective as Mr. Kipling himself could make it."
—*Boston Herald.*

"They are as true to Irish life as the songs of Tom Moore are."—*Literary World.*

"In this series of stories and studies the biographer of Father Mathew has done for Moher and its people very much what Mr. Barrie has done for Thrums in his 'Idylls.' The writer brims over with Hibernian hilarity, and his book teems with that apparently unconscious humor which is so racy of the soil."
—*Glasgow Herald.*

"A volume of gracefully written and interesting sketches of Irish life. Mr. Mathew has a delicacy of touch and a certain refinement that add to the value of his studies of Irish character." *World.*

"Ireland has found her Kipling and that is no small good fortune for her. . . . The very heart of Ireland beats in these stories. . . . There is a warm welcome in store for a dozen such books if they be as good as 'At the Rising of the Moon.'"
—*Boston Herald*

"An attractive collection of Irish stories and studies. The Rev. Peter Flannery might have been one of Charles Lever's characters. . . . All the tales are set in that minor key to which all true Irish melodies are attuned."—*The Churchman.*

"The pages bear a ripple of genuine Hibernian feeling, both grave and gay; and the printing and illustrations are excellent."—*Independent.*

"True lovers of Ireland who are homesick for the smell of the 'ould sod' will find this book very much to their liking."—*Evening Telegraph*, Philadelphia.

The Soul of the Bishop.

By JOHN STRANGE WINTER (Mrs. Arthur Stannard, F.R.S.L.). Handsomely illustrated, with frontispiece of author. Cloth, 310 pages, 12mo, $1.25. Paper, 50c.

An engrossing work which clergymen of all denominations—as well as laymen—will do well to read and carefully ponder.

In her preface the author says: "I have tried to show how a really honest mind may, and, as is, too often does, suffer mental and moral shipwreck over those rocks which the Church allows to endanger the channel to a harbor never easy to navigate at any time."

"Both theme and motive are timely, and are artistically developed."
—*Boston Daily Advertiser.*

"The book is a noteworthy protest against the retention of outgrown dogmas in the constitution of any church."—*Literary World.*

"A book of unmistakable force. The situation is perfectly natural; not an overstrained note appears in it."—*Philadelphia Ledger.*

Cheap Jack Zita.

By S. BARING-GOULD, author of "Mehalah," "Judith," "John Herring," etc. 12mo, cloth, finely illustrated, $1.25.
Paper, 50c.

Apart from his acknowledged skill as a writer Mr. Gould is the highest living authority on the wonderful fen-life in the Lincolnshire marshes, and the book is as full of strong local color as "Lorna Doone," which it somewhat resembles.

The Doomswoman.

By GERTRUDE ATHERTON, author of "Hermia Suydam," "Los Cerritos," "A Question of Time," etc. 16mo, cloth, ornamental, $1.00. Paper, 25c.

"Full of incident, passion, color, and character."—*The Critic.*

"A powerful dramatic representation of old California life."
—*Lippincott's Magazine.*

"Conspicuously superior to any novel that any Californian has done."
—AMBROSE BIERCE in *San Francisco Examiner.*

"'The Doomswoman' is an immensely clever book, and there are pages in it that deserve to live as being some of the ablest contributions to the literature of the human emotions which the English literature contains."—*Paris Figaro.*

"Mrs. Atherton has given to us a picture of the manners, social life, traditions, feuds, and ambitions of a by-gone time and a virtually by-gone race. . . . 'The Doomswoman' is not only an interesting and vivid story, but a book of permanent historical value."—*Boston Times.*

"The characters in the book are very fine. The action is rapid and interesting. The descriptions are artistic, and all is clothed with a charming style. It is a delightful book."—*New Orleans Picayune.*

"It is in the realized fulness and complex emotions of life that Mrs. Atherton's strength lies. Chonita, 'The Doomswoman,' is a character whose completeness could be surpassed by few authors. A breathing reality created by a master hand; and she is not less real because she is an uncommon, an original character. This is high praise but it is not too high."—*Vanity Fair*, London.

"The novel is full of a vivid life and personality, of freshness and fascination, of pictures which will not easily be forgotten. . . . It is by far the most picturesque and characteristic showing that has been made of that time (the old Spanish days)."—*Literary World.*

"Though Mrs. Atherton's descriptions of the land and of the estates, of the dwellings and of the inhabitants, of their christenings and marriages with the joyous accompaniments of feast and dance, are vivid and interesting, yet her novel has in it an abundance of thought, a critical intellectuality, an acuteness in character analysis that give it abundant worth even were it not placed in an attractive setting of unusual scenery."—*Public Opinion.*

"Mrs. Atherton's realism can be praised because it is natural and not pretended. Given the strange atmosphere in which her characters move, they are men and women with the virtues and failings of genuine people. Her descriptions of social life in California are vivid, and they have the effect of dissipating some of those ceremonious forms which were crystallized in much old-fashioned fiction respecting the Spaniards in America."—*New York Tribune.*

"A novel of early Californian and Mexican days before the discovery of gold. Told with force and vivid effect."—*Baltimore Sun.*

Who is the Man?

By J. SELWIN TAIT, author of "My Friend Pasquale," "The Neapolitan Banker," etc. Illustrated. 12mo, cloth, $1.25.

"The reader's interest is held spellbound from the beginning of the book to its close, and the mystery of the volume deepens with every page until the final solution comes upon him with a shock of startled surprise. The bull fight on the plain and subsequent duel are as thrilling as the chariot race in 'Ben Hur,' and the interest is never allowed to flag."—*Recorder.*

"A story which, from the opening pages to the last chapter, creates and holds the reader's eager interest."—*Philadelphia Inquirer.*

"A well-sustained story of the concealment and discovery of the authorship of crime. The action opens in Wyoming Territory but is continued and concluded on the Scottish border. The plot is thoroughly natural, and the narrative is vigorous and engrossing."—*The Congregationalist.*

My Friend Pasquale.

By J. SELWIN TAIT, author of "Who is the Man?" "The Neapolitan Banker," etc. 12mo, cloth, $1.00.

"The most noteworthy of the stories in this volume is the first, bearing the plain unpromising superscription 'My Friend Pasquale.' A most remarkable, and we might say a most brilliant, attempt to illustrate the wide range of the human imagination. The little plot has been most naturally and unaffectedly laid and faithfully conducted to a rather eccentric close. . . . The story is absorbingly fascinating and keeps one's attention actually spellbound from its beginning to its close."—*Public Opinion.*

The Lost Trader;

OR, THE MYSTERY OF THE "LOMBARDS." By HENRY FRITH. 12mo, cloth, illuminated cover. Four illustrations.

"It is wholesome and uplifting in its tone and character."—*Boston Herald.*

"A healthy and stirring romance of the sea."—*Philadelphia Press.*

"A splendid sea story of the days when steam had not yet destroyed the romance of the deep."—*Book Chat.*

"A capital story of marine adventures. Pirates, slave-traders, mutineers, desert islands, shipwrecks, sea-fights, and hidden treasures are Mr. Frith's paraphernalia and he makes full use of them all. The book will be a delight to boys."
—*Charleston News and Courier.*

"The author is a famous spinner of yarns ; there is no flagging of interest from cover to cover."—*Philadelphia Record.*

"Most picturesquely bound and well illustrated. One of the books the uprising generation will fully appreciate."—*Boston Ideas.*

The Bedouin Girl.

By Mrs. S. J. HIGGINSON, author of "A Princess of Java." Illustrated with 5 original drawings by Steeple Davis. 12mo, cloth, with appropriate design, $1.25.

"'The Bedouin Girl' is a striking story. Mrs. Higginson is one of the few white women who have journeyed with the Haj-Caravan on its holy pilgrimage, and she has done other strange feats of traveling which are seldom indulged in by American women, though English women frequently attempt them. . . . The story is decidedly original and has local color not usual in Oriental tales written by outside barbarians. . . . The description of the Pilgrimage from Bagdad seems to me capital and realistic. Not quite as gorgeous and lurid as that of the passing of the caravans in 'The Prince of India,' but very life-like.

"The Bedouin girl is a beautiful little thing and clever, and is quite a new character in the stories of these *fin de siecle* days. Her escapes are well told, and there is a decided humorous touch about the woman Ayeba who curled herself into a ball and rolled in the sand when her husband Metaah began to kick and beat her.

"Mrs. Higginson has written to entertain, and the unusual characters and scenes of her story will accomplish that object. The book makes a new ripple upon the sea of literature."—JEANNETTE GILDER in *The Chicago Tribune*.

Out of Reach.

By ESMÉ STUART. 12mo, cloth, illuminated cover. Four illustrations.

"A perfectly beautiful story for older girls, by Esmé Stuart, well remembered through 'A Little Brown Girl' and 'Mimi.' . . . The book is prettily bound and illustrated."—*Baltimore American*.

"A romantic tale which touches a bit the atmosphere of the weird, but which is in itself not the least so, being brisk and vigorous throughout. . . . The idea of the story is excellent and it is strongly handled. . . . Parts of it are very sweet, all interesting, much cleverly placed. The diction is always clear and forceful and the story, with all its romantic resources, developed amid a specially fruitful atmosphere, is one that will be widely enjoyed."—*Boston Ideas*.

"'Out of Reach,' by Esmé Stuart, is for a young girl what a novel by Mr. Grant Allen might be for her mother. . . . The book is entertaining and rather unusual in character."—*Literary World*.

Black, White, and Gray.

By AMY WALTON. With 4 illustrations. Illuminated cover. 12mo, cloth.

A story of three homes. An excellent story for children.

"It is to be recommended heartily to all who want something innocent and pleasing to add to the children's home library."—*Boston Beacon*.

"An amusing tale of three kittens and their homes by Amy Walton. It is a sensible, jolly book for little boys and girls. . . . It is not often that one comes across such a natural, sensible story so pleasantly told."—*Literary World*.

"It contains a wealth of sympathetic touches that will make each child who reads it more reflective and thoughtful in her intercourse with other boys and girls."
—*Boston Herald*.

Memoirs of Anne C. L. Botta.

Written by her friends. With selections from her correspondence and from her writings in prose and poetry. Edited by Professor VINCENZO BOTTA. A limited edition, printed on Holland paper, with gilt top and untrimmed edges. Engraved portrait of Mrs. Botta. Cloth, 8vo, 475 pages, $3.50.

"An extraordinary tribute and one that could not have been called forth by any ordinary character. Mr. James Anthony Froude, Mr. Parke Godwin, Mrs. Julia Ward Howe, Mr. E. C. Stedman, Mr. Charles Dudley Warner, Miss Kate Field, Miss Kate Sanborn, Mr. John Bigelow, Miss Edith M. Thomas, Mr. Richard Watson Gilder, Mrs. Mary Mapes Dodge, Mr. Moncure D. Conway, Mr. Justin McCarthy, and many more, have contributed these memoirs." — *The New York Sun.*

"The volume recently edited by Professor Botta, in memory of his wife, . . . will have an ennobling and uplifting effect upon all who read it, by reason of the picture it presents of an ideally beautiful life. We commend this symposium to the consideration of those ladies who are ambitious to emulate the fame of those of their sex whose names have become historical as the creators of *salons.*"
— *The Home Journal.*

"There is a touching charm about many of these memoirs; they glow with the splendor of lofty and real attachment, and they pulsate with generous and responsive life as do hearts. . . . For nearly two generations Mrs. Botta was a conspicuous force and figure in the social and intellectual life of this city. When she died Julia Ward Howe remarked, 'All her friends remain her debtors.' . . . Andrew D. White quotes Horace Greeley, who said: 'Anne Lynch is the best woman that God ever made.' . . . Froude declares that while he lives he can never cease to remember her. . . . Charles A. Peabody will remember her 'as a benefactor so long as memory shall continue to serve me.'"— *New York Times.*

"The volume of memoirs which her husband has edited is a lasting and impressive monument to her memory, builded by many hands and adorned with the affectionate and loving utterances of scores of distinguished persons who regret her loss. . . . The memoirs are most handsomely printed on heavy rough-edged paper, and are embellished with a portrait of Mrs. Botta in 'the flower of her old age.'"— *New York Mail and Express.*

"Mrs. Botta was a woman of acute intellectual insight and a most charming character. Her presence acted as a powerful stimulus in developing the social talents of others, and her 'evenings' were a recognized institution in New York, where the best writers, poets, and artists of the time attended these popular receptions. It was at one of these that Poe gave the first reading of the 'Raven.' Emerson, Bryant, Irving, Bancroft, Bayard Taylor, Dr. Bellows, the Carey sisters, Horace Greeley, H. W. Beecher, Edwin Booth, Froude, Proctor, Charles Kingsley, Matthew Arnold, Lord Houghton, and other prominent people attended Mrs. Botta's receptions, and happy recollections of these social gatherings animate the portion of this memorial contributed by her friends. . . . A portrait of Mrs. Botta taken late in life explains what Edmund Clarence Stedman said of her: 'Her grace, her personal charm, her gift of perpetual youth, were those of an ideal womanhood.' It is a stimulating book."— *Public Ledger,* Philadelphia.

"This book, commemorating a good, wise, and lovable woman, is hardly a biography, though the course of a beneficent life may be traced in its pages. . . . It is an enviable testimony to the beauty of Mrs. Botta's character and the worth of her brains that these chapters set forth. . . . What she seemed to me among the many foreigners of distinction, who have tested her hospitality in later years, is set forth in this passage from a letter written by Mr. Froude: 'I have known many interesting women in my life, but about her there was a peculiar grace which I have never seen in any other person. She had brilliant gifts, yet she never seemed to know that she had any gifts at all.'

"I was introduced into Mrs. Botta's *salon* forty-four years ago, either by Dr. Rufus Wilmot Griswold or by Mr. Bayard Taylor. Mrs. Botta, who was then Miss Anne Charlotte Lynch, was known to me before the date I have specified through her poems in Graham's Magazine and other periodicals. . . . To meet this accomplished gentlewoman was a distinction, since in meeting her one met her friends, the least of whom was worth knowing. . . ."
—RICHARD HENRY STODDARD in *The Independent.*

The Gist of Whist.

By CHARLES E. COFFIN. Pocket 12mo, red edges, cloth, 75 cents; flexible leather, red edges, $1.00.

"A valuable addition to whist literature, and must be greatly appreciated by all lovers of the intellectual game. . . . The author has examined all the standard authorities, and presented the gist of the whole subject in the least possible compass, and in the most interesting and complete and comprehensive form."
—*Evening Post*, Burlington, Iowa.

"A clever and thoroughly practical manual."—*Philadelphia Ledger*.

"A book to be bought, read, and cherished forever."—*Providence Sunday Journal*.

"Presents the chief features of the game in a strong and simple way."
—*Boston Advertiser*.

"Simple and direct in statement. The laws and leads are made clear in condensed and practical form."—*Boston Times*.

"'The Gist of Whist' meets a long-felt requirement. . . . In its one hundred pages are contained concise, readable, and comprehensive instructions of the game, under such practical heads as Fundamental Principles, American Leads, Conventional Plays, and Practical Precepts. . . . The whole is in just the shape for informative reading or quick reference. The binding, too, is dainty indeed and of itself sufficient to make one desire its possession."—*Boston Ideas*.

"A perfect hand manual of this king of card games; contains the essence of all the best guide books on the subject, including the improved method of American leads and a complete glossary of the common and technical terms, to which is added 'The Laws of Whist' as revised at the Third American Whist Congress.

> 'Know the leads and when to make them,
> Know the tricks and when to take them,
> Know the rules and when to break them,
> Know the laws and ne'er forsake them.'

"Beginners and moderate players at whist need to have the information of the game presented to them in an entertaining manner in order to awaken interest and encourage them to proceed.

"I believe 'The Gist of Whist' will possess this characteristic in a marked degree, judging from the advance sheets which I have seen. It is bright in style, and presents the chief features of the game in a strong, simple way.

"All maxims and tables of leads follow the latest and best authorities, so that the work is entirely reliable; and it is broad and comprehensive enough to graduate good players."—CASSIUS M. PAINE, Editor of *Whist*.

Barrack-room Ballads and Other Verses.

By RUDYARD KIPLING, author of "Mine Own People," "Soldiers Three," etc. 12mo, cloth, $1.00; paper, 50 cents.

"These poems are full of dramatic vigor, crisp, terse, witty, and entertaining. Those entitled 'The Betrothed,' 'You May Choose Between Me and Your Cigar' remind one of Bret Harte or Thackeray, and are alone worth the price of the book."

The Woman of the Iron Bracelets.

By FRANK BARRETT, author of "Kitty's Father," "Olga's Crime," etc. 12mo, cloth, $1.00. Paper, 50c.

"In every way an excellent story. A well-balanced, charming work of fiction, clean and bright."—*Boston Times*.

Cosmopolis.

By PAUL BOURGET. Authorized edition; handsomely illustrated by A. Casarin, a pupil of Meissonier. Large 12mo, cloth, gilt, $1.50. Paper (*not illustrated*), 50 cents.

"A work of extraordinary power and deep interest."—*Philadelphia Bulletin.*
"Bourget has given us a series of portraits which are elaborated and refined. . . . 'Cosmopolis' is an admirable piece of portraiture in all ways."
—*New York Tribune.*

The Curb of Honor.

By M. BETHAM-EDWARDS, author of "The Romance of a French Parsonage." 12mo, cloth, $1.00. Paper, 50c.

A romantic story of the Pyrenees, that peculiar French atmosphere with which that talented author alone of English writers can endow a picture of French life.
"With many and effective descriptions of scenery in the Pyrenees this story of the French and Spanish border line runs along very pleasantly."—*The Independent.*
"Grandly clear-cut is this story, harmoniously true and deeply strong. A gem cut from Nature's very *heart*, rather than from her clothing."—*Boston Ideas.*
"This story is well told and is not commonplace."—*Telegram.*
"The author shows a man, yet one full of inspiration, genius, and wit; and his great love for the waif of the storm, Eldred Eden, is exquisitely portrayed. 'The Curb of Honor' will add to the author's name and fame."—*Boston Times.*
"Miss Betham-Edwards's new book contains some excellent descriptions of Pyrenean scenery and of life in one of the remote mountain valleys on the borderland between France and Spain. Miss Betham-Edwards has made French Protestant parsonages quite a specialty of her own, and turns them to very pleasant use."
—*Athenæum.*
"The pictures of French life and scenery are fine. They belong to a field in which the author excels."—*Daily News*, Denver.

Mrs. Clift-Crosby's Niece.

By ELLA CHILDS HURLBUT. 12mo, cloth, $1.00. Paper, 25c.

This is an exceedingly piquant society novel. It abounds in striking passages, and its easy, unbroken style makes its reflection of fashionable life singularly faithful and clear. It is rare, indeed, that fashionable New York finds so gifted an illustrator as Mrs. Hurlbut.
"It is a fascinating society novel of the *fin de siecle* type. The story is really brilliant at times, with a finished, terse style that is singularly true, in detail, to the fashionable life that it describes."—*Boston Times.*
"The book is a picture of New York life; the story is well painted; clearly, smoothly, cleverly."—*Boston Ideas.*
"New York fashionable society is the subject in general and the career of Mrs. Clift-Crosby's niece the theme in particular of the present issue. Skimming lightly over the surface of life with an occasional peep into its depths, it depicts various phases of 'swelldom,' including a love affair with a French count and all the necessary adjuncts. This story will doubtless interest the summer reader."
—*Public Opinion.*
"Mrs. Hurlbut has given us an interesting picture of contemporary fashionable New York Society and has told the story of the crossed love of a wayward but very attractive and very real girl. The conception and the style of the author are genuinely artistic."—*Review of Reviews.*

The Celebrated "Pseudonym" Library.

A daintily bound and printed long 16mo pocket edition of the best new fiction. Cloth bound, gilt top, 50 cents per volume.

Every work in this world-renowned series is a literary gem, and the volumes themselves are specially adapted in size, appearance, and quality for boudoir or drawing-room use.

Vol. I. MAKÁR'S DREAM.

This is the tale of the dream which poor Makár dreamt on Christmas Eve—the very Makár who is mentioned by the Russian proverb as the step-child of Fate. The story is in turn weird, uncanny, and entrancing, and it holds the reader with wonderful fascination. Once read it will never be forgotten.

Vol. II. HERB OF LOVE. Translated from the Greek by ELIZ. M. EDMONDS.

This is a fascinating story of Greek peasant life, introducing a couple of gypsy characters and relieving them against the stolid and superstitious Greek peasantry with strong effect.

Vol. III. HEAVY LADEN. Translated from the German by HELEN A. MACDONELL.

"Ilse Frappen, above all things, paints life at first hand. She possesses the true artist's eye; and the Hamburg that could draw from Heine only the most cynical and scathing sarcasm has revealed to her a wealth of poetic material."

Vol. IV. THE SAGHALIEN CONVICTS AND OTHER STORIES.

"These stories illustrate life in a quarter of the world with which the reading public is but little acquainted. The lover of fiction will find in these pages much to delight and instruct. The scenes and characters are all novel but described with a degree of art which invests them with something of the familiarity of that which has been seen before."—*Philadelphia Item.*

Vol. V. THE SCHOOL OF ART. By ISABEL SNOW.

This story is told with wonderful verve, and yet, amid all its swing and rapidity of movement we pause at times to brush away the ready tear. It is intensely true to life, and the atmosphere is nature's own.

Vol. VI. A BUNDLE OF LIFE. By JOHN OLIVER HOBBES (Mrs. Craigie), author of "Sinner's Comedy," "Some Emotions and a Moral," and "Study in Temptations."

No work of fiction in the English language contains more brilliant writing in the same space.
The first edition was exhausted on the date of publication, and the second within six days.

"To my mind Mrs. Craigie (John Oliver Hobbes) is the cleverest of all the women who have sprung into fame within the last two or three years. . . . If Sarah Grand had Mrs. Craigie's condensation 'The Heavenly Twins' would be a much stronger book. . . . Mrs. Craigie is a cynic, and I have heard that her cynicism comes from her own experiences in life, which have not been of the happiest. . . . Mrs. Craigie is especially clever at epigram; her books are epigrammatic from the first to the last page, and in this form of literature she is much more striking than Oscar Wilde. With Oscar Wilde it seems to be a cultivated cleverness; with Mrs. Craigie it is entirely spontaneous, and is her way of looking at things. . . . The book must be read, and it will be read, for it is one of the brightest that has been published in many a long day. . . . I think that I have proved in the foregoing that 'A Bundle of Life' is well worth reading, and that Mrs. Craigie, or John Oliver Hobbes if one prefers, is a woman of sparkling though sarcastic wit."—JEANNETTE L. GILDER in the *New York World*.

"That brilliant woman who chooses to be known as 'John Oliver Hobbes' is one of the wittiest of modern writers, and her latest tale will be keenly relished for its piquancy and its clever dramatizing of a little comedy of the heart."
—*Boston Beacon*.

"The book contains a wealth of expressive word-painting, and will be warmly welcomed as one of the gems of the Pseudonym Library, which is one of the choicest series published. The Pseudonym Library represents convenient size, excellent good taste, and a nameless attraction which wins one the moment its cover strikes the view. The type is a delight to the eye, and the whole book holds a charm over the aesthetic sense."—*Boston Ideas*.

"How often in our own experiences have we found it difficult to decide whether some important change in the tide of our affairs is brought about by 'a dispensation of Providence or the interference of Satan!' And, in the society of to-day, are there not Lady Furewells and Mrs. Portenhises who can 'dress up a sin so religiously that the devil himself would hardly know it of his own making?'"
—*Philadelphia Evening Bulletin*.

"A well-written and interesting story."—*Christian at Work*.

"John Oliver Hobbes' masterpiece is clearly 'A Bundle of Life.'"
—*Boston Daily Advertiser*.

Gossip of the Caribbees;

OR, SKETCHES OF ANGLO-WEST INDIAN LIFE. By WILLIAM R. H. TROWBRIDGE, Jr. Illustrated. 12mo, illuminated cloth, $1.25. Paper, 50c.

"These sketches of Anglo-West Indian life have an unmistakable flavor of Mr. Kipling about them. . . . They are interesting bits of colony life, told for the most part in graphic, forceful style, with occasional touches of rather daring realism."—*Literary World*.

"In a succession of slight sketches or short stories Mr. Trowbridge deals with the Windward group of the West Indian Islands in its social aspects. . . . 'Mrs. Clarendon's Dance' is an excellent piece of social comedy, and there is a great deal of capital broad farce in the misfortunes that befall the ambitious hostess whose little dance proves a dismal failure. 'The Old Portrait' is a thrilling romance of the last century, which nevertheless seems to bear internal evidence of keeping pretty close to actual facts. 'For the Sake of the Cross' is a really powerful tale of noble self-sacrifice."—*Saturday Review*, London.

"The book opens out a new and unexplored region to the majority of American readers, and is intensely interesting both in style and subject matter."
—*Evening Post*, Chicago.

"The sketches are very interesting and give one a clear and comprehensive idea of the topography, climate, manners, and customs of Anglo-West Indian life in Barbadoes and the adjacent colonies."—*Town Topics*.

"These short stories contain a pleasing admixture of light satire and unaffected pathos."—*The Athenæum*, London.

Fragments in Baskets.

By Mrs. W. BOYD CARPENTER (Wife of the Bishop of Ripon). Beautifully illustrated. 12mo, cloth, elegantly embossed, $1.00. [*Just Published.*

These fragments comprise a series of twelve exquisite apologues, attractive alike to youth and age. A daintily illustrated volume admirably adapted for presentation.

Athletics as a Means of Physical Training.

By THEO. C. KNAUFF. Richly illustrated. 12mo, cloth, $2.00.

There are many text-books in every department of athletics from which one may learn rules, or how to become an expert by making a business of a pleasure. This book, however, covers the whole broad field of athletics, and with sufficient detail not only to determine the value of each pursuit as a means of physical culture, but to demonstrate what is excess and to ascertain what has been done, or what may still remain to be accomplished, by the average business man who cannot devote a lifetime to the cultivation of athletics, and who naturally desires every hour which he is able to devote to it should be one of continuous progress, and not of wasted, ill-regulated efforts, which are oft times disastrous to his physical well being.
The peculiar needs and opportunities for women in the same relation receive attention.
The work is treated very exhaustively, and in an interesting and attractive form. It has not been written from a medical point of view, but with the object of furnishing a popular work. The object has been to create a standard authority, and we think that the public will agree with us that it has been accomplished.
The volume has a wealth of original illustrations, including many life studies of great value. Some of these will appeal very strongly to those who have been neglecting the care of their own bodies, with the result of impaired health and vitality, as well as lessened capacity to enjoy life.

Americans in Europe.

By ONE OF THEM. 12mo, cloth, $1.00. Paper, 50c.

This remarkable volume, which casts so strong and at times so fierce a light on American life abroad, and the evils to which it is constantly exposed, is, beyond a doubt, destined to make a very great stir, and especially among travelers and those who are already to some extent familiar with the conditions of existence in European capitals.
The author, whose identity is only withheld temporarily, has had an unequaled opportunity of acquainting himself with his subject, and the result is a trenchant and powerful work without a single dull line within its covers. The book is absolutely indispensable to all contemplating a European residence for themselves or relatives.
A work of remarkable power. The writer is absolutely fearless in his denunciation of American practices abroad which he condemns.

"The author of 'Americans in Europe' is to be lauded for his patriotism."
—*New York Times.*

"A book that is sure to have a sale and to be talked about."—*New York Herald.*

"The author has pungent chapters on the dangers to which American young men and girls are exposed in Paris when they go there to study art and music, and mothers are warned not to send their daughters to the American Sunday-school at the French capital, that institution being denounced as a hot-bed of flirtation."
—*Boston Beacon.*

www.ingramcontent.com/pod-product-compliance
Lightning Source LLC
Chambersburg PA
CBHW031958230426
43672CB00010B/2193